W9-BHS-951

Building Bridges:
Fund Raising for Deans, Faculty, and Development Officers

Mary Kay Murphy, Editor

Council for Advancement and Support of Education

© **1992 by the Council for Advancement and Support of Education**

ISBN 0-89964-291-8

Printed in the United States of America.

In 1974, the American Alumni Council (founded in 1913) and the American College Public Relations Association (founded in 1917) merged to become the Council for Advancement and Support of Education (CASE).

Today, more than 2,900 colleges, universities, and independent elementary and secondary schools in the U.S. and 20 other countries belong to CASE. This makes CASE the largest nonprofit 501(c)(3) education association in terms of institutional membership. Representing the member institutions in CASE are more than 14,000 individual professionals in institutional advancement.

Nonprofit education-related organizations such as hospitals, museums, libraries, cultural or performing arts groups, public radio and television stations, or foundations established for public elementary and secondary schools may affiliate with CASE as Educational Associates. Commercial firms that serve the education field may affiliate as Subscribers.

CASE's mission is to develop and foster sound relationships between member educational institutions and their constituencies; to provide training programs, products, and services in the areas of alumni and constituent relations, communications, and philanthropy; and to provide a strong force for the advancement and support of education worldwide.

CASE offers books, videotapes, and focus issues of the award-winning monthly magazine, CURRENTS, to professionals in institutional advancement. The books cover topics in alumni administration, communications and marketing, fund raising, management, and student recruitment. For a copy of the catalog, write to CASE RESOURCES, Suite 400, 11 Dupont Circle, Washington, DC 20036. For more information about CASE programs and services, call (202) 328-5900.

Cover illustration by Michael David Brown.
Copyediting by Susan Hunt.

Council for Advancement and Support of Education
Suite 400, 11 Dupont Circle, Washington, DC 20036

Contents

Foreword

We are pleased to present *Building Bridges: Fund Raising for Deans, Faculty, and Development Officers,* CASE's first book on this subject. Our editor, Mary Kay Murphy, has had a long and fruitful involvement with CASE, both on the district and the national level. In 1989 she edited the CASE best-seller, *Cultivating Foundation Support for Education.* Now Mary Kay has turned her attention and her energy to the creation and development of this book on the role of deans and faculty in the fund-raising enterprise. This is a subject she has studied in detail during a career encompassing professional relationships with 18 deans in a variety of educational settings.

The chapter authors represent a variety of settings and experiences, but all speak from—or to—the perspective of deans and faculty. Deans, faculty members, development officers, and consultants—they are, as Mary Kay says, "pioneers all." In today's financial climate, we need their reflections and suggestions.

As was true in my own professional experience at Columbia University and Wellesley College, often the greatest fund-raising success arose from the collaboration and teamwork among the academic dean, a faculty member or department, and a development officer, each playing a vital role in bringing badly needed resources to the institution. Never has this teamwork been needed more than it is today. As cuts at local, state, and federal levels have helped make fund raising at public institutions the necessity, indeed the high priority it traditionally has been at privately supported institutions, the lessons in this book represent opportunities of great promise, especially for those from colleges and universities that only recently have turned to meet many of their needs from philanthropy. They will be richly rewarded by a careful reading of this volume.

The book provides a valuable orientation to the role that you and others play on the team; covers the organization and the ethics of the fund-raising effort; deals with major gifts from individuals and corporate and foundation gifts as well as those fund-raising skills deans and faculty need; stresses the essential part stewardship plays in continuing support; and looks at the role of deans in the small college and in health science centers.

I am confident that academic deans and faculty members will find both wisdom and practical assistance within the covers of this important CASE publication.

Peter McE. Buchanan
CASE President
December 1992

Preface

T he former president of Yale University, A. Bartlett Giamatti, rose through the institution's academic ranks as a professor of philosophy. During Giamatti's tenure as president, a newspaper reporter asked him what he missed about being a faculty member.

"Aristotle promised a beginning, a middle, and an end to events of importance in life," Giamatti is reported to have said. "The academic year has its beginning, its middle, and its end. Faculty members and students benefit from the cycles in that nine-month span.

"Unfortunately, administrators, including college presidents, know no such rhythms. Administrators never experience an end to their work. It just goes on and on with no end in sight."

President Giamatti's point is well taken, especially for development work in academe. Human and physical needs of the college and university are endless. Dollars required for funding are never available in great enough supply. One fund-raising campaign ends, but another overlaps or follows immediately.

The purpose of this book, *Building Bridges: Fund Raising for Faculty, Deans, and Development Officers*, is directed toward imposing a rhythm on the endless demands of the fiscal year calendar and a sense of order on the boundless financial requirements of college and university operations, especially funds for the curriculum, the physical plant, and faculty, staff, and students.

The authors in this collection are pioneers all. They have used their positions as deans, faculty members, development officers, and consultants to explore unknown territory. The initiatives they describe are, for the most, new to the annals and lore of higher education.

The chapters they offer are reflections on the paths they have taken, the goals they have staked out, the results they have achieved, the discoveries they have made, and the invitation they share with you—the reader—to join them in their explorations and path-finding.

The major focus of the book is on the dean's and the faculty member's role in development work. A secondary focus is on the teamwork and synergy that develop in the best efforts among deans, faculty members, and development officers. In these 16 chapters, the authors describe the steps they took to create an Aristotelian beginning, middle, and end in their development programs.

CASE has long been aware of the need for a book on development addressed to deans and faculty. Budget cuts at state and federal levels make private fund raising a necessity at public and private institutions. Development staffs are generally small, and they need the input and the vitality that teaming with deans and faculty gives to fund-raising operations.

Donors and prospects who are considering a large—or even a not-so-large—investment in the institution want to meet and speak with deans and faculty. Institutional needs claim top priority and call on deans, faculty, development officers, and volunteers to work together as a team in planning, coordinating, strategizing, and soliciting donors.

This book addresses several critical themes:

• the importance of institutional strategic planning and goal setting;

• the delineation of roles in the fund-raising process for deans, faculty, development officers, volunteers, prospects, and donors;

• the relationship between academic influences and success in fund raising;

• the vital need for professionalism and a sense of ethics and integrity in all aspects of the development effort.

The book is neither a scholarly treatise nor a handbook on fund-raising techniques. Rather, the authors take a close and practical look at the issues facing deans and faculty as they work to bridge the gap between the academic world and the world of the "prospect" and the "ask."

In answer to President Giamatti's lament about the lack of a beginning, middle, and end to administrative work, the book presents its content in four sections along an imagined continuum.

Section 1, "The Process Begins," addresses the initial steps of the fund-raising enterprise. Included are chapters on "Institutional Strategic Planning," "Defining Roles," "Academic Quality and Resources: Factors Influencing Fund Raising," "Cultivation and the Dean's Role," and "Building Support Through Special Events."

In Section 2, the focus turns to "The Building Blocks of Success." Here, the middle of the process is reviewed with chapters that concentrate on "Organizing for Fund Raising," "Ethics and Attitude in Development," and "New Dean, New Opportunities: A Case Study."

Section 3, "Continuing the Process to Completion," addresses Aristotle's directions for the need for closure. Here, five authors focus on "Major Individual Gifts," "Corporate and Foundation Gifts," "Involving Faculty in Development," "Effective Calls and the Art of Asking," and "Major Gift Fund Raising: The Process at Work."

Section 4, a bonus but vital section, presents "Other Considerations." "The Importance of Stewardship" focuses on what happens at the end of one gift cycle to invite the beginning of another. "The Dean's Role in Smaller Institutions" and "Health Sciences Fund Raising" present two models of specialized cooperation and teamwork among deans, faculty, and development officers at small colleges and universities and at medical schools.

As the editor of this book, I am greatly in awe and deeply indebted to the authors of the 16 chapters included in this volume. The spirit of professionalism, dedication, commitment, and sharing that they evidenced makes me one humble development officer. Their enthusiastic response to my invitation and their timely submission of copy and revisions are impressive beyond any experience I have had.

I am also deeply indebted and inspired anew by my collaborative work with Susan

Hunt, the official CASE editor of the book. I had the great good fortune of working with her on a previous CASE publication, *Cultivating Foundation Support for Education.* I have now been twice blessed to share a publication-birthing experience with her.

No greater thanks can be rendered than that which I express to Virginia Carter Smith who suggested to me that I edit this book. Further, she critiqued my outline in Montreal where she prepared to depart from CASE at the Annual Assembly. Since her retirement, she has continued to respond to my requests for help and additional content suggestions.

Vivienne Lee and Ruth Stadius of the CASE Washington staff have been great resources and helpful allies as the project moved from its nascent beginnings to publication. Vivienne Lee, vice president for resource development, gave strong leadership to organizing the annual CASE Conference on Development for Academic Deans and Faculty. Many of the authors in this book pioneered their presentations as faculty members in that series of conferences.

Ruth Stadius, director of the CASE publications program, provided continuous support to our efforts to create this publication in the world of fax machines and computer disks. Only three years separate the two publications I have edited for CASE, but it might as well have been 3,000 light years because of the revolution in publishing technology that has taken place between 1989 and 1992.

This reflection would not be complete unless I paid tribute to the collaboration that I have shared in working with 18 deans over more than a decade. These deans have headed up programs at three distinct types of higher educational models—the German scientific model, the British undergraduate liberal arts model, and the American land-grant model, Each dean has taught me something very special about his or her discipline and profession. Each has shared with me his or her dreams and plans to produce better academic or research programs. Each has made me a better development officer by bringing me into collaboration and making me a member of his or her team.

Four deans taught me very special lessons and shared with me very significant success. They are: Dean Les A. Karlovitz of Georgia Tech's College of Science and Liberal Studies; Dean C. Ronald Ellington of The University of Georgia's College of Law; Jeffrey Lewis of the State Botanical Garden of Georgia; and Provost Anthony Caprio of Oglethorpe University.

Finally, I would like to thank my mother, Eileen Erin Connors, at whose bedside I outlined this book in November 1991. My mother's life ended the day after I completed the outline. Aristotle would not have been surprised. Neither was I. During her life, my mother was my model and my inspiration for going to school and working in colleges and universities. She will remain so until my life ends. I would like to dedicate my work on this book to her.

Mary Kay Murphy
Atlanta, Georgia
December 1992

Introduction

George Keller
Senior Fellow and Chair, Higher Education Program
Graduate School of Education
University of Pennsylvania

I t is now abundantly evident that the finances of colleges and universities will grow increasingly precarious in the decades ahead. The cost of higher education in the 1980s rose about 8 percent a year while the Consumer Price Index grew about 5 percent (Hauptman, 1989). Colleges are labor-intensive and largely high-salary labor, and they are increasingly equipment-intensive; other pressures also conspire to expand expenditures.

It is evident, too, that the federal government and state governments are less and less able to support higher education adequately. In 1991-92 three-fifths of the 50 states cut their higher education budgets an average of 4 percent, with a few states chopping as much as 10 percent. Moreover, most colleges and universities now realize they cannot continue to pass their escalating costs onto students and their parents through annual double-digit tuition increases.

This means the two economic frontiers of the next decade or two will be reduced campus expenditures and improved fund raising. Universities will need to reverse the proliferation of courses, the declining teaching productivity of their faculty, the rising costs of athletics and student services, and the increased number of administrators. And institutions will need to become more strategic, aggressive, and skillful in soliciting contributions to higher education.

The traditional view has been that college presidents and their fund-raising staffs were largely responsible for collecting donations. But several developments have made this view increasingly obsolete:

• Universities especially but colleges too have been decentralizing decision making and responsibility (Zemsky, Porter, and Oedel, 1978).

• Philanthropic sources have multiplied as the number of foundations has grown, corporate giving to universities has become more routine, foreign governments and companies have started contributing, and development innovations such as deferred giving have become fertile.

• Giving for special causes and targeted efforts has increased, and knowledgeable department heads and deans are better able to solicit such gifts.

• Institutions have become more complex with honors programs, adult education programs, remedial courses, summer programs and festivals, and research institutes devoted to nearly everything from adolescent behavior to astrophysics. So the opportunities for investing in higher education have expanded, as have the potential fund-raising centers.

These and other changes require that fund raising become the responsibility of others beside the president and his or her development staff. It is now imperative that every dean at the universities and every department chair at smaller colleges become more active and accomplished in raising monies to support their operations and those of their institutional homes. It is also necessary that these new mendicants understand the peculiar priorities and solicitation style of their own campuses because fund raising can often be institution-specific (Duronio and Loessin, 1991).

Therefore, this book is both timely and useful. It will help the new legions of campus fund raisers perform more capably, wisely, and successfully. It will also assist in overcoming the extensive ignorance among deans and faculty members about the economics of higher education (Keller, 1989). In becoming more responsible for their own budgets, deans and department heads will become more astute about the largely unstudied world of higher education finance. As one dean has written, "A faculty member paid $50,000 annually actually costs the institution two to three times that amount, once one adds the expense of health and pension benefits; secretarial, telephone, postage, and equipment expenses; and the shared cost of libraries, computer technology, and administration.... Colleges have separated academic decision making from its fiscal consequences for far too long" (Lazerson and Wagener, 1992).

This volume by some of America's most thoughtful experts and deans should take its place on the desk of every dean and department chair. If its advice is followed, the book will contribute to alleviating the tightening financial constrictions that every professional school, college, and university will face in the future.

References

Duronio, Margaret, and Loessin, Bruce. *Effective Fund Raising in Higher Education: Ten Success Stories.* San Francisco: Jossey-Bass, 1991.

Hauptman, Arthur. "Why Are College Charges Rising?" *College Board Review,* Summer 1989, 11-17, 32-33.

Keller, George. "Slouching Toward Solvency: Economics as the Black Hole of Higher Education Studies," *Change,* September-October 1989, 7.

Lazerson, Marvin, and Wagener, Ursula. "Rethinking How Colleges Operate," *Chronicle of Higher Education,* September 30, 1992, A44.

Zemsky, Robert, Porter, Randall, and Oedel, Laura. "Decentralized Planning," *Educational Record,* Summer 1978, 229-253.

Section 1

The Process Begins

Chapter 1

Institutional Strategic Planning: Setting the Table for Development

Rick Nahm
Senior Vice President for Planning and Development
University of Pennsylvania

Robert Zemsky
Professor and Director
The Institute for Research on Higher Education
University of Pennsylvania

W e approach our subject with the clinking of crockery and the mingling of metaphors. We could do worse. Stewards of colleges and universities are charged with the task of nourishing their institutions while maintaining an atmosphere of domestic tranquillity. The time has come to sit down together at the conference table, which may later be converted to the dining table, and develop a strategic plan.

Learning to thrive

Good institutional strategic planning, properly understood and applied, will help you discover who you are, who you want to be, how you should interact with the rest of the world, and how you can best use your limited resources to develop your greatest potential. Caught up in the bustle of the marketplace, pressed to make choices in a changing, unpredictable world, your institution needs to set its house and its table in order to ensure stability and foster growth.

Recognizing the problems

The banquet that failed—chacun`a son gout. Fund raising in higher education has fallen victim to several increasingly apparent and seemingly inherent flaws. Most glaring of these is the distressing tendency on the part of alumni, friends, corporations, and foundations to support their own, rather than the institution's, priorities. With the best of intentions, such benefactors put at risk the character and integrity of the institution they are trying to serve. Ironically, nonstrategic approaches to fund-raising on the part of the institution—especially those that rely heavily on "leadership gifts"—inadvertently *encourage* the trend toward donor interest and away from academic need.

Loose in the candy shop—eat your broccoli! When department chairs and development officers accept gifts on the basis of what is offered rather than what is needed, they may be doing their institution more harm than good. By gobbling up everything that looks tempting and is available, they run the risk of starting unnecessary programs and buildings, which then must be completed and supported by the institution—often to the detriment of more necessary projects.

Why do I feel so hungry when I just got up from the table? Leadership gifts, although often indispensable, are high on the list of mixed blessings. Fund-raising programs, even those that appear most successful, may end up costing more money than they raise when major donors expect—and get—more than they pay for. How, for instance, does a donor get to name a building? Frequently, the privilege of naming a building goes to the donor who makes the first major or "lead" gift. Never mind that such a gift commonly provides for less than half the construction costs and none of the operating costs of the building. The hope is that the lead gift, by conferring credibility and visibility on the project, will attract further support. If, on the other hand, it happens that no one comes forward to provide major funding for a building bearing someone else's name, the institution must pick up the tab.

Having your chair pulled out—from under you. Another way donors can make their mark on an institution is through endowed chairs. The donor enjoys instant gratification when a chair is established and a professor is appointed in the donor's name. Gratification for the institution, however, is likely to be indefinitely postponed as it assumes responsibility for more than half the expenses of maintaining a faculty member and all the frills associated with the chair. Even worse is the specter of postponed-payment plans that can stretch out over years, even though the chair is filled and real money is being consumed. Such "gifts" put a high price on fund raising.

Too many cooks—there's a fly in my alphabet soup! Whether it is leadership giving that is in question, or fund raising in general, the critical questions are *who* is doing the leading and *where* are you being led. If fund raising is donor-driven rather than need-driven, what happens to institutional priorities? As areas of the institution favored by donors make conspicuous gains, straining budgets with unpaid-for commitments, faculty and students with different priorities begin to demand their fair share. Suddenly there is an escalation of expectations on the part of the entire institution, but the mission of the institution itself has become blurred. The sense of unity that makes an institution more than the sum of its parts has dissolved and "sibling rivalry" is rife.

When more is less—I demand to see the manager! As different areas throughout the institution make uncoordinated bids for support from a limited major donor pool, it may be complaints rather than funds that are forthcoming. Deluged with solicitations that do not arise out of careful cultivation and stewardship, a potential donor begins to feel exploited. Gone is the sense of family identity and unity of purpose. Made uncomfortably aware of internal strife, a would-be benefactor begins to feel less friendly toward the institution and, most damaging of all, experiences a loss of confidence in its leadership.

When the Pyrex triumph turns into a Pyrrhic victory. The conclusion of a campaign undertaken without benefit of strategic planning may leave you feeling scorched. Many sacrifices and too many promises have been made. The administration is bewildered by the discovery that the institution has more financial problems than when it began the campaign. Hostilities break out. Both donors and the campus community feel betrayed. Who is there to blame but the leaders who know neither what their institution needs nor how to go about getting it.

Feast *and* famine? The party is over. Some administrators bow gracefully out while the music is still playing and there are still gains to be celebrated. Others struggle on, not sure why all their hard work and good intentions have destroyed domestic tranquillity, strained the family budget, and obscured the mission of the institution they are trying so valiantly to serve.

An alternate approach

If you can't stand the heat—call in the caterer. Some institutions, reluctant to undertake the difficulties of strategic planning, have tried putting their fund raising into the hands of a separate, quasi-independent foundation. The foundation takes some of the heat off the administration by acting as an intermediary between specific schools or divisions of the institution and their donor communities. Under this model, no buildings or projects are initiated until the funds for construction and operating are in hand. Individual units bear full responsibility for their own fund raising. While this approach enforces a measure of financial responsibility, it puts further limitations on institutional leadership and undermines the institution's ability to serve the greater good.

Solving the problems

A menu for success—finding the right cookbook. What has been conspicuously absent from this sad scenario is the subject of our story, the Institutional Strategic Plan. The first thing to note about the strategic plan is that it has two elements, the Academic Plan and the Fund-raising Program. The second thing to bear in mind is that the Fund-raising Program arises directly from the Academic Plan and is carefully coordinated with it. The success of the strategic plan depends on the perfect blending of these two elements. It is important to understand the characteristics of each and the chemistry that makes them the perfect brew.

The Academic Plan

The missing ingredients—dishing it up. The Academic Plan should include three elements:

1. *The vision.* The first and most essential task of the Academic Plan is to create a vision of the institution that enables it to see itself collectively, to understand what it is and what it wants to be. Vision makes manifest the unique character of the institution and imbues it with a sense of identity. It supplies the language and the iconography for image-making. The process of developing a vision statement draws the institution together in a common search for unifying themes.

2. *The agenda.* The agenda is the list of proposed actions that arise from the vision statement. It is the stage at which institutional aspirations are transformed into goals. It is an agenda for action, made up of finite specific strategies for implementation. In addition, it includes measures for evaluating and assessing success or failure within a specific timeframe. While a definitive accounting of a project might be scheduled for the end of a five-year period, its progress should be constantly monitored during that time. In the same way, the overall agenda must be analyzed and reevaluated as an ongoing process. Remember, it is just an illusion that the watched pot never boils. Unless the pot is provided with a whistle, its contents may boil over or evaporate.

3. *Scale.* Scale includes a sense of priorities and limitations. Once the priorities directed by the vision statement have been identified, the institution must determine the level of investment it is prepared to commit to those priorities. Just as a kitchen scale can be useful in measuring out ingredients, scale in the Academic Plan prevents the institution from making promises it cannot—and should not—keep. Needs may be infinite, but resources are finite. Choices must be made in favor of those items that will best nourish the institution and reflect its collective sense of its own future.

Harmony and the well-balanced diet. The Academic Plan that has grown out of a coordinated sense of vision, agenda, and scale will be recognized as realistic and reasonable by the entire institution and its community of supporters. It will be accepted at both an intellectual and emotional level. Although the Academic

Plan cannot instantly accommodate the needs of everyone in the institutional community, it will reflect the ideas and the aspirations of all.

Upstairs, downstairs

We say that the ideal plan is both bottom-up and top-down in its evolution. The planning process is bottom-up in that the issues are framed from within the institution's operational units and move up through the administration to the board; it is top-down in that the board and senior administrators then refine and implement the plans to address those issues.

Getting the flavor—don't forget the seasoning. The president, deans, and other leaders responsible for drafting the initial plan must turn first to the members of the community. They must listen carefully to the views expressed by the students, faculty, staff, alumni, and friends of the institution. It is only then that they can begin the difficult process of merging the disparate voices, blending and orchestrating them into a theme that truly represents the institution as a whole. Once the vision is formed, the agenda and scale can be determined with broad participation in the actual planning process. Faculty, administrators, and trustees must all play an important role in drafting a plan that the entire institution will come to accept as its own.

The taste test—chewing it over. Once drafted, the Academic Plan must be discussed, amended, and revised, with the administration and president always bearing primary responsibility for the new draft. The final document itself need not be elaborate and should not exceed 30 double-spaced typed pages. More important than either length or attention to detail is the process by which the plan comes into being: the energy and inventiveness, the wisdom and balance, the communication and sharing that have brought the institution together as more than just the sum of its ingredients. Henceforth, the Academic Plan will provide the primary text for all institutional discussions.

The Fund-raising Program

Carving it up and forking it over. The Fund-raising Program can be thought of as the practical counterpart of the more visionary Academic Plan. It provides the tools and instructions for incisive action. When deftly employed, these tools will help you uncover all the information you need for success. Unless you were born with a silver spoon in your mouth, don't even think of digging in until you reach for the correct implement.

Choosing the silverware—the four-pronged approach. The following are essential in the development of a fund-raising plan:

1. *Developing the message.* When seeking support for anything from an annual giving drive to a major campaign, it is important to make your case with clarity and conviction. Since your fund-raising rationale derives directly from your aca-

demic planning, you have the advantage of knowing that the themes you develop will accurately represent the goals of the community. You may be confident, too, that they will find ready acceptance by your benefactors who are rightly understood to be part of that community.

2. *Setting priorities.* Fortunately, the Academic Plan makes it easy for you to put together a compelling list of your institution's priorities as determined by its vision statement. The needs and limitations that have been categorically established under the heading "scale" are now translated into specific items. With selectivity and quality the hallmarks of your choices, donors will come to see needs as opportunities and gifts as investments.

3. *Managing prospects.* This phase includes building the prospect pool and cultivating and managing major gift prospects. It ensures that fund raising is need-driven rather than donor-driven. Good prospect management begins with identifying potential donors for their interest in and loyalty to particular areas of the institution. It ensures that there will be no overlap of solicitations from competing departments. Prospects come to appreciate that they are important to the institution because they understand its needs. A potential gift is always defined by placing it in the larger context of the Academic Plan.

4. *Organizing the program.* This is the juncture at which you set timetables and goals, designate leadership and coordinate groups, and phase in new projects to be supported by fund raising. Everything from budget and staffing levels to the fund-raising timetable should be guided by the goals and objectives established by the Academic Plan.

Conclusion

The proof of the pudding—my compliments to the chef! You will know that you have set a good table if it earns the Seal of Approval from your institution's governing board. Success depends on your board's absolute commitment to the process of linking academic planning with fund raising and gifts with institutional needs. A Triple A rating from the members of your board must carry with it their enthusiastic **A**dvocacy for the Academic Plan, their strict **A**dherence to the Strategic Plan, and their **A**ctive involvement in the total fund-raising effort.

Good planning, good strategy, and good follow-through are the ingredients of successful fund raising. Before setting out on your campaign, ask yourself this question: When the bell sounds announcing that you have reached your goal, will it be the signal to come out fighting—or the invitation to sit down to dinner? It's up to you. Good luck, and bon appetit!

Chapter 2

Defining Roles: Deans, Development Officers, and Volunteers

Linda H. Gerber
Associate Vice President and Director of University Development
Duke University

Y ou have just been named dean of the College of Arts and Sciences or dean of the School of Law, and the president has told you, perhaps to your surprise, that fund raising is one of your major responsibilities. "Who, me?" you say. "What do I know about fund raising? Where do I begin? Who will help me? How can I raise money? I don't know anything about it."

For starters, don't think that you are alone. Deans often ask these questions, and you'll be in good company if you admit these uncertainties and state your willingness to learn more about fund raising early on. This chapter suggests several questions you will want to think about immediately: What is your relationship to the total university? Is your institution's fund-raising operation centralized or decentralized? Who is your team; who are the people you can count on to help you raise money? What are the strengths of the team members involved, their expectations? How will you come up with a strategy? When and where do you start?

The Chinese proverb says, "A journey of a thousand miles must begin with a single step," so let's start walking.

Where do I fit in?

One of the first things you need to know is how your school or college fits into the overall fund-raising enterprise. If you are part of a relatively small institution, this may be a simple matter—there's only one dean and you are it. The fund-raising goals and priorities you, the faculty, and the administration set are institutional ones. You work to agree on what needs to be done, and your job deals with planning and implementation.

If, however, you are a part of a complex research university with several schools and multiple development offices, the problems are different and can be compounded very quickly. For example, is your operation centralized or decentralized? That is, does your development officer report directly to you, jointly to you and the vice president for development, or some combination of the two? Do you have to adhere to any institutional policies about fund-raising priorities, prospect management, clearance, gift levels, recognition, stewardship, and so on? Whether you are dealing with a relatively small institution or a complex research university, these are issues you will want to examine carefully before you can begin to address other concerns.

What team?

"Who is my team?" you ask. "Who is supposed to help me raise all this money the president wants me to bring in to support our school?" You will discover that, like a basketball player, you are one of many on the team. The top players—the big scorer, the point guard, the captain—are you and your development officer (or officers, if you're lucky). You and the development officers are the front-line figures; you are the ones who will do the majority of the work and take responsibility for the overall fund-raising effort. Together you will make the plans, set the goals, implement the activities, ask for the money.

But don't despair. Waiting on the bench are many other people who can be key players *if* you assign them appropriate jobs and give them the assistance they need. The president can help; so can members of the administration and faculty. Think about trustees whom you can put on your team to strengthen it. Who are the strong friend, alumni, and parent volunteers who can help you make your case? What do you want these people to do for the institution? Where can you use their help?

It's your team, but you can't do it all by yourself or even with the help of your development officer. Your job is to find and use those other players who can enable your team to achieve the fund-raising results your institution needs.

What are we good at?

Any coach will tell you that one of the first things he or she does is to assess the strengths and weaknesses of the team members. You'll need to do this, and the best place to start is with yourself.

As the dean, you have many things to bring to the table. You are the school's chief advocate and representative. When you speak, you speak with the authority and the power of your office; you have credibility because of who you are and what you represent. Your knowledge is special as well. You know the faculty; you know who the outstanding teachers and scholars are. You have the academician's understanding of the school's programs, and you can explain them to a prospect far better than a development officer or a volunteer can. You have a vision for the institution's future; you know where it should be going and where the funds are needed to get it there. As the dean, you can establish school fund-raising priorities, and you must articulate them clearly to both your internal and external constituencies.

Your development officer and staff have strengths and abilities that are different from but complementary to yours. Development staff know who the prospects are for your programs, which of those you need to see and why. They can provide you with the tools for fund raising—prospect lists to review, strategies to use with potential donors, background materials on individuals you are meeting, guidance about making a direct solicitation, and suggested remarks to alumni and friends groups. And they can make recommendations on how to use these tools. Staff members are like archivists; they are a goldmine of information about the institution's or school's relationships with potential and past donors. Development officers also know the general fund-raising picture, the trends in philanthropy both nationwide and at your institution, and they will be able to make fact-based recommendations on the likelihood of obtaining private funding for your institution's projects and programs.

The other members of your team—alumni volunteers and trustees—have different strengths and, more importantly, a different perspective. They have both emotional and logical ties to your institution, and they have special relationships with other alumni and friends. Many of them have contacts to individuals, corporations, and foundations that you don't have. They may be willing to use those contacts to open doors for you, set up appointments, and endorse proposals.

If trained properly, alumni and trustees can be among your best solicitors. Never underestimate them. Many deans believe that volunteers can perform only the most menial tasks and ask for the smallest gifts; not so. Peer solicitations—one-on-one requests made by dedicated volunteers—are one of the most effective approaches to potential donors, and the right volunteer can indeed close a six- or seven-figure gift for your institution.

What should we expect?

You know what your number one expectation is: to raise more money. But on the way to achieving that objective you will need to consider other expectations—what you expect from other team members and what they expect from you.

Here are some suggestions that can help all the team members accomplish their objectives. State your own expectations from the beginning. As the dean, you have many demands on your time. Let your staff know upfront that you expect them to schedule your development time wisely; they should exercise care and selectivity in suggesting whom you will see and when. You should be properly briefed for all visits and feel confident that the development officer will do the appropriate follow-up or make sure it is done. You expect the staff's best professional opinion about fund-raising priorities, goals, and strategies for achieving those goals. You expect to be prepared, but never programmed (as in a wind-up toy). You need to be kept informed, and never, *ever* do you want to be blind-sided because your staff has left you in the dark.

Your development staff will have some expectations as well. First and foremost, staff expect to be full members of your administrative team. Include them in dean's council meetings (or whatever your administrative advisory group is called) so that they'll get the complete picture of what's occurring at the school. Development officers also want to know that you consider them professionals and will treat them as such, taking seriously their advice about whom to see, what to ask for, and what strategies to use.

Second, staff expect you to stick by your time commitment. If you have promised to make calls on a particular day, don't cancel at the last minute unless you have an excellent reason. To do otherwise may damage your own credibility as well as that of your staff.

Staff also want decisions and expect some consistency in working toward fund-raising priorities and the goals that have been set for achieving those priorities. Changing direction in midstream will certainly have a negative impact not only on staff motivation and performance, but also, and more importantly, on desired fund-raising results.

Finally, your staff will expect you to make a personal dollar commitment to the school. This is critical! Making a gift yourself not only makes it easier for you to solicit the gifts of others, but also gives you credibility with your internal and external constituencies.

Volunteers are there because they choose to be. Never forget that they have many other organizations for which they could be working. Thus it's imperative that you ascertain what they want from you and what they can do for you in return. The biggest mistake fund raisers make with volunteers is not signing them on when they offer or, worse still, giving them busywork. Volunteers expect to be treated like professional staff members; they need good, solid job descriptions that outline their tasks and provide clear explanations of how their work will be evaluated. They need to be assured that you will train them well, not just paper them to death. They need to be used wisely, rewarded well, and recognized appropriately.

And you need to consider how to move the best volunteers up the institutional volunteer ladder. If they do a terrific job, can they be appointed to another committee or a board of visitors? What can you do for them? You and your development officer will need to think long and hard about who your best volunteers are—or could be—and how you can fulfill their expectations.

Plan, plan, plan

The title of this short section says it all. In later chapters in this book, you will be given more detail about the planning process. But it's important even in this brief overview to emphasize the value of planning.

From your very first day on the job, you and the development staff should allow time for thinking: What do you want to accomplish and how can you do it? Where are you going? What are your goals and objectives? Who can help you achieve those ends? Your entire team—you, the dean's council, your administrative staff, your development personnel—should be part of this process. You need to think about both short- and long-term plans and develop a timetable for each. What do you want to accomplish right now, in the next three months? six months? Where do you want to be five years from now? How will you determine whether or not you have been successful?

Establish realistic and achievable goals, both for dollars and for the activities necessary to achieve those dollars. Encourage your people to think big and to think positive. Keep in mind that this should be big as in ''stretch'' rather than big as in overwhelming. When you and the team finish putting together your plan, you want everyone on board and committed to what can be achieved. Exercise the kind of leadership that inspires confidence in the mission of the institution. Plan, plan, plan. Nothing can be accomplished without this critical step.

Conclusion

Building your team, assessing your strengths, addressing expectations, planning—all these things are extremely important. But the time comes when you and your team need to stop thinking and start doing. At some point, setting to work must take precedence over formulating big-picture ideas and planning strategies.

Finally you need to take the first step—recruit the first volunteer, identify the first prospect, make the first visit, ask for the first gift. This book will help make those steps easier.

So go to it. Keep walking on that thousand-mile journey.

Chapter 3

Academic Quality and Resources: Factors Influencing Fund Raising

James J. Boyle
Associate Vice President for University Advancement
State University of New York at Binghamton

How does the college classroom relate to the charitable checkbook? Why should concerns of deans and faculty about academic quality issues be shared by development officers? In higher education, fund raising and the academic enterprise are inextricably linked. The quality of an institution's academic program is a major influence upon its ability to garner financial support from its alumni. Alumni support also indirectly affects the success of the institution's corporate and foundation development programs.

Surprisingly, many faculty members view development as something others do—the nonacademic "hired hands" employed in college and university administration. This misconception is unfortunate, because faculty members play an important role in influencing institutional capacity for engendering external financial support. Therefore, fund raising cannot be understood, or be successful, if it is perceived as an isolated process, divorced from the educational mission of colleges and universities.

Academic influences on giving

This important relationship between academic strength and development success was documented in my recent study of alumni giving and college quality, a research project supported by the Lilly Endowment (Boyle, 1990). In the study, alumni giving was selected for analysis because of its importance as the largest donor category in support of higher education (over 25 percent of all funds donated annually) and its impact upon other donor groups (e.g., leveraging additional foundation and corporate grants).

Not only are the personal gifts of alumni significant in financial terms (over $2 billion annually), but they serve as a symbolic affirmation of the institution's work and as one measure of graduates' satisfaction. As President Charles Eliot of Harvard remarked at the turn of the century, "It is not merely what alumni give; it is the fact that they do give that is of supreme importance" (Stewart, 1955).

In the study, as the key measure of alumni satisfaction, I used participation rate in annual giving, rather than the dollar amount of alumni gifts. This made it possible to control for the differences in giving capacity and socioeconomic status of alumni from a wide range of colleges. I surveyed 300 private liberal arts colleges (randomly selected) and averaged their annual alumni participation rates over the 1976-1986 decade using data from *Voluntary Support of Education* (Council for Aid to Education). The mean alumni participation rate was 23.4 percent, but ranged from a low of 4 percent to a high of 61 percent averaged over the decade.

The study sought to determine what factors, particularly academic, influence the propensity of alumni to give to their alma maters. Would those alumni who experienced higher quality education be more likely to give? Using a combination of correlational and case-study research methods, I selected a dozen quality and resource proxy measures to provide a quality profile of each institution. I used measures from nationally published sources in the 1960s in order to portray institutions as large numbers of alumni would have earlier experienced them (American Council on Education, 1968).

Prerequisite for giving: A sound educational program

The study found high correlations between alumni participation in giving and four important indicators of institutional commitment to providing a strong academic program. (In the following, "r" symbolizes the correlation coefficient, a measure of strength of association, the value of which can range from minus one to plus one. A minus one indicates a perfect negative correlation, while a plus one indicates a perfect positive correlation. Zero means there is no relationship between two variables.)

- the number of library volumes per student ($r = .55$);
- average SAT scores of entering freshmen ($r = .55$);
- the percentage of faculty holding doctorates ($r = .54$);
- the educational and general budget per student ($r = .54$).

More moderate correlations, but nevertheless significant, were found between alumni giving and

- the endowment funds per student;
- the college's admissions selectivity;
- the student-faculty ratio.

Further examination of these correlations through multiple regression analysis produced a somewhat different mix. The best predictors of alumni giving to colleges in this analysis were:

- library books per student;
- average SAT scores;
- student-faculty ratio;
- endowment funds per student.

These four measures of college quality and resources were able to explain 44 percent of the variance in alumni giving among the 300 colleges in the study. These data indicate that colleges that focus their spending priorities on faculty, instruction, libraries, and other academic quality investments should expect a higher rate of alumni contributions.

Other motivators of alumni giving

At the outset, the study used quantifiable data to measure college quality and resources, but it was hypothesized that nonquantifiable factors might also influence the propensity of alumni to respond favorably to appeals for financial support. What other factors might account for the 56 percent balance of variance in alumni giving among the colleges, not explained by the regression analysis?

To answer those questions, in-depth case studies were done on high- and low-performing "outlier" colleges (two colleges where alumni giving exceeded their predicted rates, and two where it did not reach the prediction). (An "outlier" is a case (i.e., a college) with scores that differ remarkably from the general pattern established by other subjects in the sample. In multiple regression analysis, an outlier indicates actual performance (i.e., in alumni participation rate) either far above or far below the predicted score.)

Unfortunately, only those colleges with strong quality indicators agreed to participate in the study and to receive visits. The few colleges that reported high alumni giving rates and low quality would not agree to campus visits in spite of guarantees of anonymity and confidentiality. Furthermore, in the few years since the initial study data were calculated, the two underperforming colleges experienced dramatic increases in alumni giving and nearly achieved their predicted rates.

Importance of faculty

The case studies of the four colleges used a variety of research techniques, including document analysis and extensive interviews of alumni, trustees, presidents, faculty, and development staff members. The principal finding of this component of the study was the major role played by faculty members in the alumni development achievements of the colleges. College presidents, provosts, and deans agreed that an outstanding faculty was essential to an academic program of high quality, but it was the many graduates interviewed who overwhelmingly offered "the faculty" as the key determinant in their motivation to give financial support to their colleges.

Nearly a universal response in alumni interviews was that the strong influence of faculty members was a dominant motivator of alumni loyalty. Whether described as "a great teacher," "an inspiring mentor," "a prominent but caring scholar," or "a lifelong friend," a faculty member of the high-quality case study colleges was the primary influence on the graduate's decision to donate to the institution.

A generous alumni trustee of a college that consistently leads the nation in alumni participation in alumni giving put it this way:

> Most people go away feeling they owe a debt to the college. Our high giving percentage is due to the great regard for the school—the feeling of alumni that they got a bargain. They want to pay something back. The closeness with the faculty fosters that. Faculty become students' friends. You know that the faculty are still back there in the trenches, and it's a little way of repaying them for what they did for you.

These faculty-student relationships were not one-sided, however; the faculty members interviewed in the case studies described their associations with students as personally rewarding. They said that a high-quality student body helped attract outstanding teachers, just as a good faculty brought in better students; one reinforced the other. Faculty members expressed satisfaction with their frequent out-of-class interactions with students (as club advisers, special event participants, research project colleagues, and dormitory advisers), and that these rewarding experiences later carried over into faculty members' frequent visits to regional alumni club meetings as guest lecturers.

Campus cultures: Community and bonding

The colleges that had successful alumni giving exhibited other common characteristics, in addition to a high-quality academic program, which alumni defined primarily in terms of an outstanding and caring faculty. Well-organized and well-financed alumni relations and alumni development programs, supported by the presidents and the trustees, were important factors in the success of the case study colleges. Faculty at these colleges were not disdainful of fund raising or reluctant to accept volunteer outreach assignments; indeed, faculty involvement in alumni programs was frequent.

Campus cultures that fostered a sense of community were also common to the successful colleges. From the first day of freshman orientation to later involvement in alumni activities, graduates spoke of their "bonding"—their sense of belonging to the college family—which inspired a lifelong obligation to support the institution. The more distinctive the college, the stronger the community ethos, which was reinforced by traditions, rituals, residential life, and the age of the college.

Perhaps surprisingly, fraternities, sororities, and athletics had only minor influences on alumni loyalty. Integration of students into both the academic program and out-of-class campus life helped strengthen the institutional bonding. And philanthropy awareness programs, which educated students during their undergraduate experience about their future obligations as alumni, reinforced appeals for financial support after these students had graduated.

Study implications for deans and faculty

Correlations do not prove "cause and effect," but merely show associations or strength of relationships. Therefore, investing in strong libraries, excellent faculties, and students of high ability will not suddenly guarantee colleges a wellspring of new alumni contributions. This study *does* indicate the important relationship of academic quality to success in alumni development at 300 private liberal arts colleges, but just what do these findings mean on the practical level?

Budget priorities

At most colleges, academic deans and faculty members are seldom the primary financial decision-makers. But they can utilize their important roles in college budgeting, strategic planning, and faculty senate committees through dialogue with other institutional leaders to ensure that libraries, student-faculty ratios, educational and general spending, and searches for qualified faculty members receive priority attention. Greater involvement of deans and faculty in the recruitment effort can improve the search for high-ability students through the admissions program.

Student contact

Deans and faculty members involved in personnel searches can see to it that excellent teachers receive priority consideration; the value of community building through close interaction with students can be assessed in candidates' past positions. Faculty committed to an active research agenda might be persuaded to involve students in their scholarly investigations as research assistants. Administrators and faculty members can volunteer their time and expertise to serve as club advisers or faculty masters in residence hall programs. Institutional leaders can use incentives such as release time, tenure and promotion, and recognition awards to encourage the faculty to become involved in interactions with students.

Alumni program involvement

Despite the many competing pressures for the out-of-classroom attention of faculty members, deans and other academic administrators can facilitate closer working relationships between faculty and alumni and development offices; the rewards may be significant and immediate. Faculty lecturers who volunteer to speak at regional alumni club events often meet potential significant donors, who may be more willing to discuss their personal situations with faculty than with administrators or development officers. Deans' newsletters to alumni can stimulate readers' interests in particular academic programs or innovations, and this can lead to major and often unanticipated financial support.

Similarly, the alumni development office may be aware of well-placed graduates whose corporate relationships or networks among private foundations can lead to grants for faculty research or academic program enhancement. Alumni advisory councils, jointly organized by academic administrators and alumni development officers, help to garner not only new financial support, but useful advice from past recipients of educational services. For example, when alumni were interviewed for the study, they expressed a strong desire to assist their alma maters, not only financially but also through involvement in many other aspects of the college. Indeed, many alumni respondents resented being asked only for their financial support and contributions.

At larger institutions where it is more difficult for alumni to relate to the college as a whole, outreach programs by deans and schools can strengthen the graduates' "old college tie" to the smaller and more familiar units with which they are more likely to identify.

Conclusion

Fund raising for higher education is not done in a vacuum. What goes on in the classroom directly influences the success of the fund-raising program. The study documented the fact that commitment to academic quality pays financial dividends over the long term. Nearly 40 years ago John Pollard reached a similar conclusion in a study for the Council for Financial Aid to Education: "The first principle of fund raising for any college or university is that it should carry on a sound educational program. Tinsel does not attract gold. A belief in the quality of an institution, and in the importance of what it is doing, is the main motive for contributing to it" (Pollard, 1958).

That belief in the institution's quality must be instilled during the students' years on the campus:

> It is really too late, of course, to woo an individual if you wait until [he or she] is an alumnus. The time and place to develop alumni loyalty is during the undergraduate years on the campus. The student who has had good teachers, is given wise counsel and helpful individual atten-

tion, and is oriented to a sense of obligation and responsibility during [his or her] college career is generally the student who becomes a staunch old grad (Pollard, 1958).

This research project demonstrated that alumni development is not simply a matter of "tugging at the heart strings to open the purse strings." Even the most productive professional fund raiser today will not succeed if the alumni did not appreciate the quality of the academic experiences provided during their undergraduate years.

The study also showed that the recipe for alumni reciprocity requires more than the judicious investment of resources in the faculty and other academic priorities. The quality of the institutional development program and of student life outside the classroom also plays an important role in engendering alumni loyalty. And finally, deans and other institutional leaders need to remember that colleges do not raise money for the sake of having money. The alumni participation rate and the funds raised by the annual fund should be viewed in their proper perspective— as means to educational ends. The institution that applies increased alumni financial support toward those quality enhancements will find that more support from today's students will be generated in the years to come.

References

American Council on Education. *American Universities and Colleges* (10th ed.). Washington, DC: 1968.

Boyle, J.J. "Grateful Graduates: College Quality and Alumni Giving." Unpublished doctoral dissertation, Syracuse University, 1990 (UMI #9119415).

Council for Aid to Education. *Voluntary Support of Education.* New York: 1976-77, 1980-81, 1985-86, 1987-88.

Pollard, J.A. *Fund Raising for Higher Education.* New York: Harper, 1958.

Stewart, E.T., Jr. "Alumni Support and Annual Giving," *The Annals of the American Academy of Political.and Social Science,* 1955, 123-138.

Chapter 4

Cultivation and the Dean's Role

Joseph M. Zanetta
Executive Director, External Affairs
School of Business Administration
University of Southern California

Jack R. Borsting
Dean
School of Business Administration
University of Southern California

A s dean of an academic unit, whether at a major research university, a liberal arts college, or a specialized school, you play a leadership role in development. The dean is the primary spokesperson for the institution's academic programs, and he or she must articulate the goals and objectives of the school or college. The university president and provost are ultimately responsible for the academic goals of the institution, but in these times of financial stress in higher education, they cannot be expected to focus significant efforts on one professional school or college. The dean, working with the faculty and staff, must develop a vision for the school; articulate it to the external world; somehow attract the attention of the media, alumni, and business community; and focus energies toward those individuals capable of supporting the institution with a major gift. A dean is expected to obtain philanthropic support that will help the institution reach the next level of excellence.

Cultivation is an important part of the development process. Obtaining philanthropic support from individuals, corporations, and foundations requires sophisticated interpersonal skills, knowledge about the prospect, and a commitment to the academic mission of the school. Every school has a natural constituency—the students, alumni, faculty, staff, professional colleagues, and friends of the school. It is up to the dean and his or her development staff to determine how best to build bridges with the various stakeholders that will result in the securing of external funding for the academic program.

Events and publications

A natural way to develop interest in a program or school is to be out in the community discussing the academic program of the school. A medical school dean should attend and be a speaker at the local AMA meetings. A law school dean should become active in the local bar association. A business school dean has perhaps a wider range of opportunities, since business spans all areas of economic activity. Professional school deans have a natural constituency in their profession. Deans of arts and science schools, however have a less well-defined population to work with and develop.

Public events—either sponsored by the university or by a local service club—are important ways to state the institutional message. The dean needs to "work the crowd" at those functions and be properly staffed to follow up with individuals who show an interest in the school. The goal of public events should be to help the dean and development office identify a group of individuals and funding sources that require further involvement with the school. In development parlance, the "cultivation" process is a series of steps that bring those individuals closer to your institution. While the ultimate goal is to secure a gift for your school, the dean and the school's development staff must first involve the major gift prospects with the school. And each of these prospects will require different kinds of attention.

Your institution should provide a wide array of activities to involve prospects. Guest lectures, lunches with an outside speaker, and receptions are a few of the possibilities. An alumni reception at a bank or corporation is an excellent way for the dean to meet employees who attended the university or college. It also provides an introduction to the CEO or senior executive of the corporation.

Your own school publication—whether it is a newsletter, tabloid, or glossy magazine—provides a wonderful opportunity for you to state the mission of the school. The school publication should be distributed to all stakeholders in the external constituency, as well as to internal faculty and staff. It should include messages about the school—its students and faculty accomplishments—as well as comments about the current state of the discipline. The message can discuss strategic issues, such as globalization of the program, or it can focus on a professor who has received an award or made a discovery. The message should convey sincerity and academic integrity, for it will help inspire prospective donors to support your institution with a gift.

Speeches, receptions at football games, and other kinds of special events can reach hundreds or even thousands of individuals. An alumni magazine may be sent to even more alumni and friends. The dean has to understand that the public events and printed word are important in building enthusiasm for the program. However, the cultivation of major gift prospects should focus on only 10, 20, or perhaps 30 individuals. No one person can properly cultivate hundreds of prospects. If the dean is committed to securing gifts for capital purposes such as an endowed chair or a classroom building, he or she, working with the development staff, must identify those individuals who are able to make a significant impact on the school through a major gift.

Only through proper use of the dean's limited time will he or she be successful in developing relationships with those individuals, corporate executives, and foundation trustees who will look favorably upon a formal request for financial support. Like a political campaign, events and publications develop excitement, enthusiasm, and a positive "spin" for the school in the community. The dean must always remember that an academic institution needs to articulate its goals.

Prospect research

Consultants who conduct feasibility studies usually analyze the school's prospect base in the hopes of determining how successful a major capital campaign would be. Computers and access to national databases now make the task of obtaining research information on prospects less complicated although yielding more data.

Why conduct research in the first place? Studies of philanthropy show that wealthy individuals usually make major gifts to institutions for a variety of reasons: Belief in a cause, institutional loyalty, the desire to honor the memory of a loved one, the need to establish a personal legacy, and involvement by peers. As dean of a school, you need to know if a wealthy alumnus' widow would wish to honor his memory by a gift to the school or would prefer to invest in cancer research, the disease that claimed her husband's life. It is important to understand the theory of what motivates an individual to make a major gift before you begin the research process.

Many development officers, in good faith, make the mistake of obtaining tremendous amounts of research on the prospect's financial capability. Evaluations of a prospect's financial capability will help you avoid soliciting too small or too large a gift. However, with the technological revolution in information retrieval, you can learn a great deal about the donor's financial status. Annual reports, SEC filings, census data, and corporate prospectuses provide a wealth of financial information.

What is more important is information about the prospect's interests and relationship with your institution. An alumnus' feelings toward the alma mater may change over time, but fundamental beliefs do not. For example, a wealthy alumna who is adamantly opposed to a recent change from a women's college to a coeducational institution has taken the institution out of her will, no longer makes annual gifts, and has written to the president that she no longer considers herself an alumna. Does it matter that this woman is extremely wealthy? Probably not. It appears highly unlikely that she will make a major gift to an institution in which she no longer believes.

Other feelings change over time. An alumnus may withdraw financial support after his or her child is rejected by the institution or even after an important football game is lost. However, proper cultivation of these prospects may bring them back into the fold. Research on individuals should ascertain their attitudes toward the school, their involvement with the school over time, and their intellectual and academic interests.

Many deans forget that individuals provide nearly 90 percent of the charitable gifts reported in the U.S. Corporations and foundations often seem to be easier targets of opportunity because they publish annual reports and provide guidelines on their philanthropy. A wealthy individual, unless he or she has established a charitable foundation, does not make it so easy to determine philanthropic interests.

This is where information-gathering becomes of tremendous importance. After a personal visit, the dean and the school's development staff should immediately record their observations and all the information they obtained. Development officers must develop systems to record information on prospects. Word-processing and various software programs make this quite simple. After a visit, the dean or development officer should write a memorandum to record whatever information was discussed.

If the wealthy widow stated that her prime interest is to honor her husband's memory, that should be recorded in the expectation that a suitable proposal will be developed. In fund raising, the dean must be a good listener. The prospect often sends out signals in subtle and not-so-subtle ways about the desire to support the program with a gift. It may not be appropriate for the dean to solicit the prospect on the first contact, but it is necessary that the dean make a written record of the visit with the prospect.

In major universities, a variety of academic programs and schools seek support from the same source. A law school alumna, for instance, may have an undergraduate degree in business from the same university, while her husband attended the university's medical school. Both of them are music patrons. The business school, law school, medical school, and music school could all legitimately attempt to solicit the couple. This is where deans and school development officers must be team players even while they are promoting the interests of their school. It often requires astute political skills to obtain an official university clearance to solicit those prospects who have many interests.

If a dean visited with this couple and learned that their goal was to help eradicate cancer because they had lost a child to the dread disease, it would probably make sense for the medical school to approach the couple about a gift. Information of this kind is more important than how many shares of General Motors common stock the couple owns. Of course, without information about such indicators of wealth, the couple would not even be considered as prospects. But interests, commitment to a social cause, or the desire to honor a deceased family member's memory is ultimately more important than a financial statement in determining if the major gift solicitation will be successful.

Information can be obtained from a variety of sources. Usually, the donor is the best source. Once the dean has established a friendship with the prospect, he or she should be able to ascertain what program the donor would be interested in supporting. A donor's friends, family, attorney and accountant, neighbors, and classmates often provide an interesting perspective and insight on the major gift prospect.

Ethical issues in research

Some in the academy think it is improper to do research on prospects. A fundamental premise is that an educational institution must operate at all times in a manner consistent with the governing board's philosophy. If the president and the board of trustees have endorsed academic programs and have determined that it is appropriate to seek external funding, it is the dean's responsibility to execute a development plan. There is nothing unethical about trying to learn not only about a prospect's academic interests, but also about his or her financial ability to make a major gift.

Ethical considerations arise when overzealous fund raisers invade a donor's privacy. The university's right to know about its alumni and their financial capability should not trespass on the individual's right to privacy. Some financial information is already in the public domain, such as proxy statements, annual reports, initial public offering prospectuses, and real estate holdings. In our view, there is nothing inappropriate about analyzing those public indicators of wealth.

On the other hand, serious ethical questions would arise if family financial records required for financial aid reasons were used to determine potential for making a gift. In fact, this seldom occurs because most families who apply for financial aid do not have the resources to make a major gift.

Ethical problems may occur when researchers use sensitive financial information obtained in an unusual way. An accountant or attorney, for example, may have significant financial information about a prospect. However, the attorney-client privileged relationship precludes sharing detailed financial information with others. Research should focus on donor interests, hobbies, and affiliations with professional associations so that the institution can attempt to match a donor's interest with the academic program. The use of volunteers to assess a donor's wealth and interest is perfectly appropriate.

Sometimes a prospect may have obtained his or her wealth in an unethical way. There have been well-publicized examples of institutions that suffered public relations problems after accepting a gift from an individual with an unsavory business reputation. This is always an extremely difficult issue that must be analyzed by the academic leadership of the institution on a case-by-case basis.

If there were a litmus test applied to philanthropy, many of our largest gifts would have to be declined. Major foundations such as Rockefeller, Carnegie, and Ford were the creation of individuals who had controversial reputations in their time. It is more difficult to accept a gift if the donor is alive and has a reputation as a corporate raider, or violated federal law, or was indicted (but never convicted) of a crime. Once again, the dean, and probably the governing board, should establish gift policies and standards as to gift acceptance. In some cases, it might be inappropriate to accept a gift.

The role of the dean and faculty

The dean and faculty members play a pivotal role in the cultivation process. Individuals who are interested in supporting the educational institution with a major gift need to be inspired by the great teaching and research that are taking place. Every school or college should have programs that are unique or special. Alumni may wish to establish a scholarship fund in honor of a favorite professor. Corporations often have deans and faculty members serving on their boards of directors. When an academic serving in such a role retires from an institution of higher education, it is a fitting tribute to ask the corporation to establish an endowed professorship or scholarship fund in honor of the retiree.

Faculty members are often overlooked in the cultivation process, as well as in the identification stage. A dean usually serves for a finite period of years and often comes to the institution from another college or university. Tenured faculty members normally make a lifetime commitment to the university and thus develop over time an institutional memory. Having faculty members with an understanding of the institution's culture, history of philanthropy, involvement with wealthy students, and community activities can be extremely useful to a new dean. After all, most alumni base their impressions of their alma mater in large part on the experiences they had in the classroom. Certain faculty members feel that it is the dean's job to raise money, and *they* shouldn't be bothered. The dean should attempt to educate faculty members to their important role and interest as many as possible in fund raising.

Some administrators feel that using faculty members as fund raisers is risky because they are only interested in obtaining gifts and grants for their own programs. While this is sometimes a legitimate concern, the dean should encourage gifts to all programs. The dean and development officer should be able to harness the faculty members' enthusiasm and contacts to generate additional external funding for the college or program.

A dean is not effectively introduced to prominent alumni and business leaders simply by being appointed to the position. He or she will need help in obtaining access to these important contacts. Senior faculty are usually well-positioned in the community to open doors for the new dean. Faculty often establish such contacts through their stewardship responsibilities; a faculty member who holds an endowed chair usually visits with the donor or the donor's family on a periodic basis. These stewardship visits are appropriate opportunities to introduce a new dean; cultivation of past donors assures their future gifts to your institution.

Some deans have their own development staff. Others work with staff from central development. The dean should utilize his or her staff to do research, staff functions, brainstorm donor strategies, and make sure cultivation is followed up.

Role of advisory boards

One of the most effective ways to obtain a voluntary commitment to your school or college is to ask the prospect to serve in an advisory capacity. Most people like to be asked for their advice and counsel and appreciate the opportunity to serve on some type of voluntary board. Throughout our society, men and women serve as volunteers in churches, community organizations, nonprofit organizations, schools, colleges, and universities.

In higher education, most active volunteers and alumni realize that governance is vested in the board of trustees. It is the board that has a fiduciary duty to see that the institution is well-managed financially, and the board also appoints the chief executive officer. Beyond governance, however, there are numerous opportunities for involvement. A dean must be willing to have a group of individuals who offer constructive suggestions and who do not always agree with him or her. A thoughtful dean will assemble a group of men and women who are bright, collegial, and interested in the school's programs. These groups go by many names—Visiting Committee, Board of Advisors, Board of Councilors, External Review Committee, Task Force, Ad Hoc Council—but all serve the same purpose: providing advice to the academic programs and leadership of the institution.

Some boards have as part of their responsibility the solicitation of gifts. Others are composed of individuals who wish no role in fund raising. Whatever the composition of the group, the dean should realize that involving people in an advisory manner provides excellent cultivation. Wealthy individuals need to believe in an institution or cause before making a major investment in the program. Advising about a new program, reviewing curriculum changes, debating the issue of going coeducational or opening an office in Tokyo are exciting forms of involvement. Deans should provide volunteers with an intellectually stimulating forum designed to assist the school in reaching the next level of excellence.

An advisory board can be set up for an academic department, a research center, or for a temporary ad hoc situation. Sophisticated individuals understand that they do not have governance responsibilities, and some of them understand that the dean may be seeking their wealth in addition to their wisdom. In any event, such advisory boards are strongly recommended. Faculty members make excellent additions to certain boards.

The charge to the advisory board should be made clear at the outset—in writing. Some boards have fund raising as their primary focus. Others do not offer any commitment to development assignments, but instead provide interaction with students and faculty. The partnership between alumni and business leaders and faculty and students creates benefits for both the university and the business community. Corporate executives often seek faculty members for consulting work, and faculty may use visitors to lecture in class. Alumni and corporate executives make outstanding guest lecturers for an occasional class or on an adjunct basis. The interaction is very valuable. Faculty and the dean, however, must always realize that once the advisory members have left campus, the actual implementation of the plan depends on them.

Conclusion

The dean of a professional school, college, or academic program has a vital role in the cultivation of major gift prospects. He or she sets the tone for the institution and is the embodiment of its academic goals and aspirations. A dean should view special events and publications as a way to tell the institution's story to the outside world. Research on potential supporters is helpful in the cultivation process.

To be successful with a donor, there are three fundamental principles: follow up, follow up, follow up. The school's fiduciary duty to the donor includes an obligation to see that the donor's goals are implemented. Ultimately, the major gift will occur if the donor believes in the academic programs and leadership of the institution.

Chapter 5

Building Support Through Special Events

April L. Harris
Public Relations Consultant
Houston, Texas

D eans who are successful at fund raising rely heavily on an organized,
year-round series of special events to attract potential donors. Special
events are those occasions to which an institution or organization invites
outsiders for a closer, more personal look at facilities, programs, policies, and staff
than is generally afforded on a daily basis. Special events can include annual hap-
penings, such as a homecoming open house for the college's alumni, or they can
be unique one-time occurrences, like a lecture and autograph session with a visiting
author who is an alumnus of the institution. They can take place on your campus or elsewhere.

Special events can be small and directed toward a very specific audience, such
as a dean's tour and luncheon for a select group of community leaders. Or they
can be massive in scope and directed toward the general public, such as ceremonies for the dedication of a new academic building.

Special events are key elements in a comprehensive public relations plan that
deans and development officers have designed to advance institutional goals in
community relations and fund raising. They bring people, resources, and messages
together to accomplish specific objectives.

Whether private or public in scope, special events put your college or university on display and offer people the opportunity to look at and, indeed, scrutinize
the institution and its programs. Powerful communicators, special events send messages that make a far more lasting impression than the most expensive brochure
or eloquent plea for donations.

Because special events are so potent, use them wisely. They can yield maximum
results in terms of both friend raising and fund raising, but only if they are stra-

tegically positioned in the long-range goals for the advancement of your institution. Do not create special events in isolation, but weave them into your total development program so all activities complement each other.

What is the role of special events in fund raising?

A balanced special events plan should include a mixture of two kinds of events: those intended for "friend raising" and those intended for fund raising. Especially if you are just beginning to use special events as a component of your institution's development plan, it is important that not all events be fund raisers. People will lose interest if they perceive that every time your institution sponsors an event they will be asked to donate money.

The major objectives of a solid special events plan should be to build goodwill, educate your audience about your college or university, and create an awareness of your institution as an important resource. Referred to in fund raising as "cultivation," these friend-raising activities require varying amounts of time and attention in your overall development plan depending on the relationship your institution has already established with its constituents.

If there have been no outreach programs in the past, you may need to spend time in friend raising before you can begin fund raising. On the other hand, if your institution already has an active involvement with alumni and other constituents, you may be ready to sponsor a fund-raising event and meet with great success.

"People give to people" is an axiom in fund raising. Special events enable you to reach out to your publics on a personal level in order to build support for your institution by creating an awareness of quality teaching, research, students, and programs and by highlighting the accomplishments of your graduates. By making friends while simultaneously educating constituents about your college or university, you are building bridges and laying the groundwork for future political, volunteer, and financial support.

Friend-raising special events are an integral part of your long-term development plan and can be simple and low cost. For example, you might establish an "executive-in-residence" program through which selected alumni return to campus (at their own expense) to deliver guest lectures and meet with students, faculty, and administrators.

Once you become actively involved with your constituents through special events, you will find a more receptive audience when fund-raising appeals are made. In the current climate of increased competition for philanthropic dollars, institutions need to be perceived as indispensable members of the community, worthy of support.

Making a master plan

How do you determine what kinds of events to sponsor and how often to sponsor them? Careful planning is the key to success.

Special events must be solidly anchored in a mission-accomplishing strategy or your efforts and your money will be wasted. There is one valid reason to sponsor a special event: to support and enhance your institution's goals and mission, thereby contributing to the accomplishment of objectives in public service, image building, and fund raising. Random events held for the sake of a one-day success can send mixed messages to your audiences and sap resources that could be used more effectively in a well-planned public relations program.

Special events are a powerful tool in your public relations kit. Therefore, when you plan goals and objectives for the coming year and develop public relations strategies to accomplish them, you should also develop a master plan of the special events that will be part of your overall development program.

This must be done on two levels: First, determine the institution's goals and objectives and then examine overall institutional public relations and events plans. In this way, you can help assure that your efforts will not duplicate those of other groups, center on the same audiences, or be trampled in a crowded schedule of campus events. This information will often suggest ways to dovetail your ideas into the existing plans, thus maximizing chances for success and increasing the impact of dollars spent.

On many campuses prior to the start of a new academic year, the chief public relations officer convenes a meeting of representatives of offices that typically plan events. Included are staff from alumni, development, athletics, admissions, student activities, and the president's office. This meeting is a roundtable discussion in which each group describes its plans.

As the dean, you should send a representative to this campuswide meeting to gather information about institutional priorities and goals for the coming year and to find out about major fund drives, awards, construction plans, sports schedules, and special projects. This is a good time to confirm dates for major functions, such as commencements, convocations, concerts, parents' day, and breaks. This information can help avert planning disasters—such as scheduling an important event that depends upon student involvement on the same date as the largest fraternity and sorority event of the year.

Armed with a sense of the big picture for the coming year, you can proceed with developing your own campuswide special events master plan. Refer to your goals and objectives to make a list of what needs to be accomplished; leave the "how" until later in your planning process. For example, your "what" list might include recognizing a major donor, increasing statewide awareness of your institution to improve student recruitment, and educating alumni about cramped conditions in your present facility.

Now, match goals and objectives, and review your "what" list to look for logical tie-ins with your target audiences. For example, you may have learned that on a certain Saturday the alumni office will hold a day of activities that will involve several key alumni. You might take this opportunity to schedule an "alumni faculty day" for the preceding Friday. Share this information with the chief public relations officer.

Pencil in dates that seem attractive. Consider the availability of staff and facilities, especially on weekends that are already busy. Will essential suppliers, like caterers and equipment vendors, be spread so thin they won't be able to handle your event effectively?

Think about the people you want to involve. Will they be able to attend your event and give it the attention it deserves? Check the calendar carefully to make sure the date you are considering is not a religious holiday or Super Bowl Sunday.

Now, get specific. You've analyzed the big picture and zeroed in on probable dates. What should you plan? Think about each project's significance in your total development plan and how it will fulfill the specific goals you have set. If you carefully tailor each activity to draw attention to the facilities, people, and programs that set your institution apart, you will increase attendance at your event and make a long-lasting impression on those you invite.

Getting specific

Follow a few basic principles when deciding on the theme or type of event you will sponsor:

Consider your target audience. Are they young or old, students or professionals? Are they affluent or on a shoestring budget? Are they frequently in contact with your campus and your institution, or will this event be their first exposure in a number of years?

Think about the unique features of your institution. Do you have unusual collections or other resources, such as a planetarium, a gallery, or laboratories, that could be the focus of a special event?

The events you choose should be appropriate to and compatible with your institution's mission and image, and they should fit into the school's annual public relations plan. Therefore, before agreeing to plan and hold a special event, ask yourself these questions. Does the event:

- support the institution's mission;
- help achieve specific goals;
- showcase resources unique to your college or university;
- help friend raise or fund raise;
- build goodwill;
- consistently comply with the institution's image; and
- match available resources?

If the answer to any of these questions is "no," scrap the idea and rethink the conditions that gave rise to it. Ask yourself: Why do we think we need a special event? What do we hope to accomplish? Is a special event the most effective tool to fill the need?

Fund raising on campus

Today virtually every college, university, and private school conducts organized fund-raising activities and has a professional development staff to plan and manage

32

them. Before implementing any fund-raising efforts, coordinate your plans with your institution's development office. Chances are you will find the staff to be an invaluable source of support and advice to help you achieve success.

The development staff can help you identify potential donors and determine their probable level of giving. They will also steer you away from prospects who have been targeted for other contributions or who are being cultivated for major gifts to other areas of the institution. It is important to respect this advice to avoid sending mixed signals to potential donors and thus jeopardizing fund-raising plans that will ultimately benefit all.

Because the development staff are involved with many special events throughout the year, they are a good source of advice on maneuvering through the logistics of planning and implementing a successful special event.

Making the plan a reality

You've developed a master plan, selected dates and themes, and determined exactly how to use a special event to communicate to your target audiences. Now you must deal with financing and promoting the event, planning the details, working with volunteers, implementing the event, and following up.

First, build a budget based on research. By their very nature, special events fall outside of the traditional budgeting process. Events not only change from year to year, but can sometimes grow from modest to grand, seemingly overnight. Funding needs also vary. One manager may be more resourceful than another in securing donations to underwrite special events. The projected cost of an event may fluctuate, ticket sales may fall short, or the decorating committee may overshoot its budget by 50 percent. Budgeting for special events is frequently a process of calculated, educated guesses.

If you use your master planning exercises, you should be able to build a fairly accurate budget proposal. To do this, estimate the costs of each event, including:
- facilities;
- equipment;
- security;
- entertainment;
- invitations and program printing;
- postage;
- food and beverages;
- extra help;
- speakers' fees; and
- travel expenses.

Don't just pull numbers out of the air. Telephone local vendors to get estimates for each item or service.

Depending on the budget process at your institution, you may be able to acquire funding from several sources. Additional outside funding may be available from your alumni association or foundation. Working with your development office, you may be able to identify potential underwriters or corporate sponsors.

A word of caution: *Never* approach an individual, corporation, or foundation to underwrite or to sponsor a special event without clearance from and coordination with your development office. This office may have a proposal in the works or pending before the potential sponsor. You don't want to endanger a larger, more important gift to your institution by not doing your homework. At the same time, you don't want other proposals coming in later and competing with yours. The development office can save you from going down blind alleys, offer approaches to your potential sponsor that are based on experience in dealing with the individual or organization, and sometimes suggest alternative sources of support.

Underwriters and sponsors

Underwriting and corporate and foundation funding offer ways to cover some or all of the expenses of an event. These arrangements may allow you to offer the event to the public free of charge, reduce ticket costs, or increase your "profits." They may also provide a cushion in case your event is not a success.

Sponsorship can take the form of goods and services. A beverage company may be willing to provide soft drinks; a local print shop may agree to print your programs or invitations. Again, work with your development office to avoid stepping on toes and to identify alumni and local business people who may be able to contribute goods and services that will help defray expenses. Most contributions of this nature are tax-deductible, but don't promise deductibility until you have cleared this with your development office.

Corporations become event sponsors because it helps to enhance their image as good corporate citizens. Most sponsors are very interested in public recognition, such as having the corporate name and logo printed on event materials. Plan ways to recognize your sponsors, but always clear public recognition and all uses of the corporate name and logo with corporate sponsors before you release any publicity or have any materials printed.

In addition to whatever event recognitions you offer, the development office may provide others, such as membership in established university giving clubs. The development office or your institution's foundation is responsible for issuing official gift receipts and therefore must be kept closely apprised of your sponsor agreements.

Getting people involved

Whether your special event is a friend raiser or a fund raiser, working with a committee and volunteers will result in the greatest flow of ideas and the widest exposure for your event. A committee enables you to tap into the creativity of several people with varying points of view and gives you an entree to the business and social circles of committee members. Well-chosen committee members with good connections can open doors for you.

Enlist the participation of the leaders of your target audience to give your event stature and credibility. But don't select someone only for his or her name or position. If a person cannot make a specific contribution to the committee's mission, don't invite him or her to serve. You owe it to yourself, to the other committee members, and to your event to assemble the most active, creative, productive committee possible. By the same token, don't ask busy people to serve on a committee if you don't plan to use their advice, talents, and time.

A few basic guidelines will make working with committees easier and more productive:

• Establish a clear set of goals and objectives for the committee.

• Decide beforehand who will chair the committee and run each meeting.

• Distribute a written agenda at the beginning of each meeting and stick to it. Limit circuitous discussion and argument.

• Take minutes at each meeting and distribute them as soon as possible.

• Make sure meetings begin and end promptly and are run efficiently.

• Respect your committee chair as a professional and always be forthcoming with information related to the project.

If your college has an active volunteer or "friends" group, special events are a fun, productive way to give them meaningful involvement. Using your volunteers to help plan and implement special events brings several benefits: You reduce overhead by eliminating some labor costs; you give people the satisfaction of knowing that their volunteer time is being spent productively; and you take advantage of another avenue of access to potential new donors and influential community circles and members.

Volunteers are an excellent source of talent and labor: They can make decorations, design printed materials, round up supplies such as tables and chairs, serve refreshments, greet guests, act as tour guides, and give demonstrations.

Special events and liability

Unfortunately, there are always risks involved in special events, and you will need insurance. If you are hosting a small event on school property, your regular insurance will probably cover you in case of an accident (a guest slipping on the entry tiles, for example) or misfortune (a guest's fur coat being stolen). But in many other cases, your event will not be covered by insurance.

Questions of liability become sticky when you serve alcohol or when you are sponsoring an event that will attract a large crowd, such as a festival. Even hiring a bus to shuttle guests to and from parking lots requires a check on coverage.

Consult your institution's risk manager or insurance agent early in your planning to determine any special coverage you might need. In most cases, a rider—a temporarily stipulated set of conditions—can be attached to existing policies on an event-by-event basis.

Determining the coverage needed, finding an insurer to write the policy, and calculating the size of your premium all take time, so contact your institution's risk manager early. You may find you have to alter your plans if coverage is unavailable or too expensive.

Making your event work

Think small. Success hinges on the details, and coordinating the hundreds of details involved in a special event is an enormous task. Whether an event is small or grand in scale, the sequence of decisions is essentially the same:

1. Be certain that the purpose of your function has been clearly defined.
2. Identify the goals and objectives of the event.
3. Develop a fairly accurate idea of the number of people expected to attend.
4. Select an appropriate facility that is compatible with your budget.
5. Make an outline of all the elements involved, from promotion and registration to audiovisuals and insurance.
6. Determine the theme, colors, and decoration scheme.
7. Decide on food, beverages, and entertainment.
8. Prepare a minute-by-minute order of events.
9. Plan the billing process and follow-up procedures.

The number one secret to success is good communication. You can't do it all alone. Good solid planning involves hours of brainstorming, explaining, selling, and coordinating to make certain everything and everybody wind up in exactly the right place at exactly the right time.

To accomplish this, delegate as many details as possible to the experts in each area, and keep the communication flowing between yourself and the committee, caterer, florist, entertainers, printer, campus VIPs, maintenance staff, equipment rental firm, security personnel, and anyone else who has a role in the event. Good communication conveys an important message—it tells the people involved how important they are to the success of the event and, in doing so, it increases their commitment to your project.

Promoting the event

You can plan the best event in the history of your institution, but it won't come off if the people you expect to come don't know about it. Publicity is vital, and different kinds of events require different kinds of publicity.

An invitation-only, black-tie fund-raising gala requires a minimal amount of pre-event publicity—perhaps a photo in the local paper with the committee chairs announcing the date and purpose of the event.

On the other hand, if your event is a community open house that will feature displays, demonstrations, and an exhibit of illustrations drawn by area school children, you will need a good deal of publicity. On some campuses, a story in the alumni magazine will generate a sell-out crowd.

Publicity is the art of creating excitement about your special event, not only among members of the working press, but in the minds of the target audience and the community in general. Publicity requires research, planning, and careful attention to detail.

From a newspaper editor's point of view, most college and university special events are not news. You're more likely to receive publicity after the event through coverage of celebrities who appeared, photos of ribbon-cuttings, or mention of a large donation from a local donor.

For these reasons, it is important to entrust your publicity efforts to the professionals on your institution's PR staff. These specialists can help determine your needs, write news releases, take photos, and supervise the distribution of information to appropriate media outlets. The PR staff will save you an enormous amount of time and can also spare you embarrassment because they have a good sense about what kind of stories the local media are likely to use.

Publications for the event

All publications related to the event—invitations, response cards, tickets, decorations, promotional fliers, posters, menu cards, programs, souvenir items, and so on—should have a uniform graphic theme that is expressed though color, paper, type, logo, and design. Everything should match. Work with your institution's publications staff or a graphic designer and printer to develop a package to fit your budget for the event.

Evaluating the event

After the event is over, don't yield to the temptation to push it out of your mind and move on to another project. You have one major hurdle to be cleared: determining whether the event accomplished its original goals in the context of the institution's big picture.

Did it draw the intended audience? Was the intended message clearly and decisively delivered? If it was designed to encourage donations, did it provide enough information and foster enough goodwill to make potential donors receptive when a development officer calls or an appeal arrives by mail?

If the event was poorly attended or didn't generate the funds you had hoped for, ask people you trust to give you an honest assessment.

Schedule a final committee meeting to review the event and take notes on members' reactions. While the details are fresh in your mind, write a chronological review of the event with comments about what was good and what was bad and what you might improve. Keep this report on file with all the financial information pertaining to the event. You can use it to avoid repeating your mistakes the next time you are planning the same or a similar event.

With thorough planning and careful follow-up, you can make your special event an enjoyable, productive tool for building goodwill and achieving your institution's fund-raising goals.

Section 2

The Building Blocks of Success

Chapter 6

Organizing for Fund Raising

Curtis R. Simic
President
Indiana University Foundation

T hat people contribute their time and resources is a remarkable and price-less gift to higher education. Giving is a complex process, one that originates in the heart and enables people to foster and nurture the institutions and values they cherish. Through giving, donors and volunteers perpetuate the excitement of learning, opportunities for personal growth, the benefits conferred on society by research and the arts, and the chance to influence for the better those who will shape the decades to come.

We have a responsibility to enable those who want to give of their time and resources to do so. In so doing, we must make a commitment that equals theirs: We must create a carefully thought out and executed organizational structure that, by its professionalism and integrity, encourages success in the institution's overall advancement as well as in fund raising.

As is true of most major initiatives, success depends on a commitment from the top down to make development a priority. Implicit in that commitment is the inclusion of your institution's chief development officer on the team of top administrators. Fund raising is an integral part of the institutional advancement effort, and it is vital that the development effort be a part of planning and decision making at the very highest levels. Further, it is vital that you as dean be aware of and promote the need for all areas of your institution or academic unit that deal with external constituencies to be committed to working together. These include alumni affairs, development, community or university relations, grants and sponsored programs, athletics, and admissions—an area in which contact with the institution's constituents is usually quite extensive.

Successful fund raising is based on the long-range plan for your institution. No institution can organize its fund raising in the most effective way unless the institution has a comprehensive, far-sighted, and dynamic plan, one that outlines its mission and goals and delineates the objectives that will enable it to reach those goals. In the process of agreeing upon goals, the institution and you as dean must look at the institution's organizational strengths and weaknesses and at the environment in which it is operating and will operate in the coming years. In developing such a plan, the institution must have consulted its constituencies, both internal and external. These likely will include deans, faculty, administrators, students, staff, donors, volunteers, alumni, parents, corporations and foundations, government officials, and friends.

Once the institution's long-range plan is in place, the basis for effective fund raising is in place. Not only are the perceptions and realities, as well as the strengths and weaknesses, that are uncovered in the planning process vital pieces of information for the development operation, but also—and most important—the fund-raising plan is based on the institutional plan. I cannot overemphasize this: The institutional mission is always primary; fund raising priorities must reflect what the institution seeks to accomplish to fulfill that mission.

Setting priorities: What should we raise money for?

As a dean, never make ad hoc or piecemeal decisions about what projects to take on. Always base the decisions about fund-raising priorities on those institutional priorities identified by the long-range plan. If there is no long-range plan, become an advocate for one. In the interim, utilize accreditation plans or seek funding for institutional Strategic Plans.

The actual process of determining fund-raising priorities should consist of a series of carefully defined steps that gives each constituency an opportunity for input so that decisions are considered and informed. An example of steps in the priority-setting process is as follows:

1. Actively encourage suggestions from all your constituents for programs and projects that will further your mission. These suggestions must derive from the institution's long-range plan, as supported by the unit submitting a project.

2. Forward these suggestions to the chief academic officer of your unit, who will review them and send them on to a committee appointed by the president or chief academic officer of the institution. The committee should include representatives of the administration, deans, faculty, grants or sponsored programs office, the development office, and perhaps students. The mission of the committee is to select projects that support the long-range plan.

3. Determine the cost of each project. The cost must be realistic and must include an inflation factor.

4. Set up a grid with your list of projects on the left-hand side and possible funding sources across the top. Funding sources might include:
- operating budget;
- capital budget;
- special project grants;
- federal grant and overhead monies;

- student tuition;
- special student fees;
- private support from annual gifts;
- private support from special or campaign gifts.

Assign each project a source or sources of support.

5. Forward to a second committee a list of projects that are assigned wholly or in part to private support categories. Like the first, the members of this committee are appointed by the president or chief academic officer of the institution and include members of the administration, deans, faculty, fund-raising professionals, and perhaps students. The committee should be chaired by the president or chief academic officer.

6. The fund raisers then conduct a feasibility study for these projects. This study assesses the attitudes, assumptions, and perceptions of those who have been, or are expected to be, key volunteers or donors. The feasibility study asks four questions of the respondent:

- What is the institution's overall capacity for raising funds?
- What is the potential for raising funds for this project?
- What effect will a campaign for this project have on other projects?
- What resources of the institution will be required to mount a successful fund-raising effort, and what will it cost to provide these resources?

7. At the same time, you need to assess your own readiness, whether it be that of your academic unit or of the institution as a whole, to participate in the fund-raising process, particularly if you are planning a special project or major gift campaign. Ask yourself these questions:

- How does the project goal compare to the annual giving total? The rule of thumb is that the goal for a special project or major campaign should not be more than 10 times greater than your annual figure.

- How does your program rate against others? What honors have the faculty won, and how well are they regarded by others inside and outside the profession for their teaching, research, and service records?

- What about your pool of prospects? Do you know who they are? Do you have a way to assess their affluence and their sphere of influence? Do the gifts you receive now come from a well-balanced variety of sources including alumni, other individuals, corporations, foundations, and other organizations?

- Is the head of your program, school, or institution willing to allot up to 30 percent of his or her time to fund raising? The head must take a leadership role and be willing to commit budget, clerical support, travel funds, office space, and other resources to support the fund-raising effort.

- How willing is the faculty to be involved? Faculty are, after all, the experts in most areas for which fund-raising campaigns are developed. Will they be willing to help develop or review proposals, meet with donors who want to understand and share in the excitement of their program or project, or perhaps accompany a staff member or volunteer on a fund-raising call?

- How are the costs of fund raising to be covered? Can the necessary expenses be funded by unrestricted gifts? If not, can you find an alternative source of funding?

8. Once this information is obtained, the leadership—whether that be you as the dean or the governing board of the institution—can make a decision about the readiness of the unit to conduct or participate in the process and the feasibility of achieving the fund-raising goal.

9. Of the projects that meet all the requirements, the leadership of the unit or the institution chooses those that will be undertaken by the development office.

Now that we know what we want to do, how do we do it?

Centralized vs. decentralized fund raising. Most fund-raising operations begin as small, perhaps even one-person, offices. As the institution grows, so does the development office until eventually the institution may decide that size, complexity, and changes in management style and institutional organizational structure make the creation of multiple development offices a possibility. The "centralized" development operation becomes a "decentralized" one in which development officers reside in their academic units, but the central office continues to handle certain functions.

Strong arguments can be made for and against both the centralized and decentralized structures. A central development office that faces the same budget constraints as everyone else may not have the resources to add enough fund raisers to cope with all the development needs of a large institution. Fund raisers who are based in a central office are usually assigned to several schools or departments and may not know any one of them as well as a fund raiser based in the academic unit itself might.

Deans who are committed to fund raising often prefer to have development officers based in their academic units, reporting to them and directly accountable to them. Most donors, usually more than 95 percent, designate their gifts for particular purposes. Having a development officer in the unit often creates for those donors a closer and more personal link with the institution than a central development officer could create. A development officer in the unit can also communicate more regularly and easily with faculty whose daily tasks of teaching, research, and service often make them the most eloquent spokespeople for their institutions.

Yet there are some aspects of fund raising that are more easily and efficiently handled by a central office, and this is why almost all systems, even those called "decentralized," still have a central office.

Almost everyone agrees that it is important to have a central place to enter and maintain records and to record gifts. Also important is a central office that tracks and manages the prospective donor pool. Few situations are more embarrassing to an institution than having three or four development officers, faculty members, or deans show up on a prospect's doorstep within a few days of each other to talk about different projects. It will be obvious to the prospect that little or no thought has been given by the institution to how to best approach him or her.

Some services realize economies of scale through centralizaton. For example, few units need their own full-time attorney or planned giving officer. Other services can also be centralized. Researchers, whose materials are becoming more and more expensive, can collect a vast centralized library of information sources and use them to compile information on prospective donors for any unit. A publications staff can specialize in fund-raising materials for all those in development.

Centralized accounting can provide tight and consistent controls over the gift accounts and the expenditure of gift funds. When investments are handled collectively, units with little to invest can pool their funds with larger units and thereby realize a greater return. Specialists in corporate and foundation fund raising can offer their expertise to unit development officers when needed.

If units are short on travel funds (and they usually are) and if the central staff has regional assignments, they can make calls on behalf of the units in the areas they are visiting. Centrally coordinated mailings and phone programs reduce costs and improve efficiency for everyone.

Centralizing some management and organizational structures benefits the institution. It's important that all those working for the institution discuss and agree on certain issues such as criteria to be met before launching campaigns, feasibility studies, expenditures of gift funds, and investment strategies. The institution should have established policies and procedures that enable it to retain its credibility and achieve those efficiencies that make development productive.

There are general institutional needs and priorities that only a central office can address for the institution as a whole: student programs that cut across all disciplines, general scholarship and fellowship aid, projects that have been designated as priorities for the institution as a whole—projects that have an institution-wide impact.

Often no unit development officer could handle such priorities. Perhaps the department that has a project with institutional priority has no development officer, or the development officer does not have the time, resources, or expertise.

The central development staff is, in effect, the president's fund-raising staff. Alumni belong to the institution first. The institution, not the department or school or campus, confers the degree. The central development office can provide consistent recognition and stewardship services for all of the institution's supporters and keep before alumni the vision, accomplishments, and contributions of the institution as a whole, without threatening their loyalty to their department or school.

In her 1989 dissertation, "A Comparison of Decentralized and Centralized Patterns of Managing the Advancement Activities at Research Universities" (University of Maryland), Margarete Rooney Hall described the pros and cons of centralized, decentralized, and semi-decentralized systems in schools of business and engineering at research and doctorate-granting institutions. Her research was based on extensive surveys and interviews with presidents, chief advancement officers, deans, and, whenever possible, development officers. Hall found a trend toward decentralization; she reported on respondents' opinions as to which responsibilities should be centralized and which left to the academic unit development officers; and she found a strong correlation between the organizational structure and managerial culture of an institution and the structure of its development operation. For those in comparable institutions or those whose development programs are evolving, Hall's research into trends and management issues will be very useful to deans, faculty, and development officers.

My own experience is that the structure of the fund-raising operation usually does reflect the structure of the institution it serves. Highly centralized institutions usually have a highly centralized fund-raising operation. At the other extreme, an institution with several campuses, each managed by a highly independent chancellor who gives the deans great latitude, usually has a highly decentralized system.

There is strong evidence that the most successful fund-raising programs—the most productive, progressive, and highly regarded—are highly centralized or have established a high degree of coordination between a strong central development organization and development officers in the units.

In-house development or a separate foundation? The development operation can be a major contributor to the success of the department, school, or institution, whether it is a part of the institution or a separate foundation. I believe, however, that effective operations are enhanced by having a separate foundation.

A separate foundation that is a not-for-profit corporation offers special advantages to fund-raising operations, especially those at public institutions. Through a separate foundation, gift funds can be kept separate from other monies. This is important for several reasons.

First, it enables you to protect the confidentiality of your donor records. Major donors often provide half or more of your gifts every year, and they have shared personal correspondence, wills and trust agreements, and other sensitive materials with you. They give these materials to you in trust; you cannot violate that confidence by allowing these materials to be accessible to the public or the press.

Second, a separate foundation offers the academic institution flexibility in expenditures. Many institutions, including public ones, are asked to budget one to two years or more in advance and have little flexibility once that budget is set. Gift funds can offer deans and faculty members the resources to take advantage of the opportunity to buy a new piece of equipment that has unexpectedly come on the market, to offer a fellowship to an outstanding graduate student, to make an award to their brightest undergraduate, to offer research support funds to faculty, and for myriad other uses.

Some institutions limit certain kinds of expenditures, such as faculty relocation expenses—the very expenditures that might enable the institution to attract the most outstanding teachers and researchers. It is important that there be some other source for these funds, such as a foundation.

Keeping your gift funds in a separate foundation has advantages when it comes to investments too. Some institutions are limited by statute in the ways they can invest public funds. Foundations are strictly regulated too, but they follow different rules and can often achieve a return on investments that is more than the institution can realize if investment vehicles are limited to bonds, for example. This can mean a difference of thousands or millions of dollars a year in resources for your institution.

A separate foundation is organized specifically to be responsive to the needs of donors and the development function. Donors and prospects require education, legal guidance, personal attention, accounting procedures that go far beyond what is required by law, and stewardship. The development office itself requires ways to track prospects and donors and to evaluate its own productivity, among other special needs. A separate foundation can be the most responsive to donors and to the special requirements of fund raising.

Finally, a separate foundation expands your opportunities to make "insiders out of outsiders." Through recruiting and involving board members and consulting members of board committees and other volunteers, you can greatly expand the number of people who understand your institution and its priorities and can represent those to their friends and associates. As their involvement with the institution and the fund-raising process deepens, these new insiders find their commitment to the institution and its success deepening. They become allies of and advocates for the institution.

Selecting foundation board members and other volunteers for their affluence, influence, and the degree to which they represent your constituencies along geographical, racial, and gender lines, makes your institution and development office more representative and more responsive than politically appointed boards.

Directors and other volunteers should also be chosen for their expertise. Their experience and knowledge in particular fields enables them to do substantive work for you and at the same time establish a strong and enduring connection with your institution and its future.

Responsibilities

The fund-raising operation, whether it be in-house or a separate foundation, has a responsibility to exhibit the highest degree of integrity. It is important to put in place the tightest controls on every part of the process—recording and acknowledging gifts, authorizing expenditures, internal and external audits, and so on.

At the same time, the fund-raising operation needs to provide as much information as possible without violating donor confidentiality. Fund raisers have an obligation and a duty to inform those they serve. Formal and informal reports to the institution and to donors are critically important. Do an annual report, make your investment policy statements available, release your audit report, publish your expenditure guidelines, and be open about your sources of funding and operating budget. Communicate with all those involved in development for your institution. The strongest fund-raising operations are those that communicate.

How do we pay for fund raising?

It's true: It costs money to raise money. Every institution faces the inevitable question of how to pay for professionals and support staff, the recognition dinner, the computer time for recordkeeping, travel, phone calls, and the thousand and one things that are necessary to support the fund-raising effort. It is what William Boyd, president emeritus of the Samuel Johnson Foundation, calls "the intractable issue of the relationship between money and quality."

Ultimately, there are only two sources of funding: the institution and gifts (or earnings on gifts). Some development offices within a department, school, or smaller institution might be funded entirely by operating monies from the unit or institution. Large, independent foundations might have to work out more complex formulas, combining a variety of funding sources.

The institution might contribute to the fund-raising office by a direct allocation of operating budget funds that derive from tuition, fees, income from auxiliary enterprises, or, at public institutions, the state appropriation. A separate foundation might enter into a contractual arrangement with the institution it serves and receive a fee for its services. Departments, schools, or campuses might be assessed a fee for the use of centralized fund-raising services such as account management, prospect research, publications, prospect tracking, feasibility studies, legal services, investment management, check writing, recordkeeping, donor relations, and data processing.

Some institutions levy a charge against incoming gifts, taking a small percentage to help cover the costs of the fund-raising operation. This approach spreads the charge out over all gifts and distributes the cost over all the units receiving gifts. It is also a one-time charge. An alternative is to take a percentage of the return on gifts that are invested. This places the burden on units that have invested funds, and the charge is levied repeatedly.

No solution will make everybody happy. What should make the decision makers happy are the results.

And this is why it matters...

Fund raising is an almost magical area where you can see extraordinary generosity and caring for people, issues, and institutions. Donors bring their higher selves to their gifts, and they use them to express the values and beliefs that are most important to them. Your responsibility as dean is to respond with an organization that equals in its integrity, clarity of purpose, and effectiveness the care and thought and concern that the donors are expressing when they make their gifts.

Chapter 7

Ethics and Attitude in Development

Frank T. Read
Dean and Professor of Law
University of California
Hastings College of the Law

T he new dean approaches the first major donor proposal meeting with the enthusiasm of a dental patient facing a root canal. Why the trepidation? Deans are frequently selected because they have achieved a high degree of academic acclaim as faculty members. They see the task of deaning as a natural progression in a distinguished academic career, a platform where they can exercise their academic leadership skills to achieve great advances for the college or university.

Shortly after warming the decanal chair, however, the new dean faces reality: Money is the fuel that runs the institution, and without money the dean's great dreams for academic achievement will never come true. And at last comes the realization: Fund raising is part of this new job—an essential part.

The mindset problem

While most deans accept this truth, many view it with distaste. If you are in such a position, take heart; fund raising can be fun. Believe it or not, fund raising can be one of the most challenging, ego-rewarding components of your job. It's all in your attitude, the mindset with which you approach the task.

Your first fund-raising venture may be somewhat like going fishing for the first time. You get up at an unreasonable hour on a rainy morning just to sit in a drafty boat on a foggy lake. Hours pass while you put wiggly live things on a hook and sit and wait for something to happen. Does this sound like fun? Then the line jerks, the fight is on, and soon you are landing your first fish. You forget all of the preparations—the early rising, the long drive, the cold and the damp—but you remember forever the thrill of the catch.

Think of your first fund-raising expedition as a first trip out on the water. It's not much fun at the beginning—it may seem downright painful—but it may turn out to be an unforgettable experience.

New deans often dwell on how difficult it is to ask somebody for big dollars, but if the preparation has been thorough—the professional fund raisers have done their work well and the prospect has been appropriately cultivated—you can approach your part of the task with confidence.

As dean, what you are really selling is a vision of the future of your institution—an institution in which you believe and to which you have devoted your career and perhaps a good part of your life as well. You do have a good product to sell!

The harrowing moment arrives, you make the dollar request, and fortune smiles. The prospective donor agrees to pledge a large gift to your institution. And you thought catching that first fish was a thrill, but this is a thrill that lasts; the money you have raised will go into a fund to enhance the quality of your institution in perpetuity. Generation after generation of students and faculty will benefit from your work. This is a thrill that will grow into a lasting satisfaction.

Fund raising can be fun. But to do it right you have to have your head on straight. You have to approach fund raising not only as an essential part of your job, but also as one of the most satisfying. If you approach it with fear, foreboding, and distaste, your success rate will probably be pretty low. And you will not be the dean you hope to be.

Ethical sensitivity

Once you begin to view fund raising with a little less dread, perhaps even with the rosy glow of hope, it's time for some more realism. Fund raising is not without its headaches and its heartbreaks. Sometimes, in the eagerness of the chase to obtain a major gift, we overlook the traps that may be encountered along the way. Let's call these traps "ethical pitfalls." Ethical pitfalls, whether obvious or hidden, can cause greater problems than you ever dreamed.

As important as it is to raise funds, there are some gift situations and some donors you should avoid from the start. Remember the haunting line from the pop tune about Maggie Mae—"I wish I had never seen your face"? Over a long career of many major gift proposals and achievements, almost every experienced fund raiser has cause to feel that way about some donors whose gifts contained ethical pitfalls that might have been avoided with a little forethought.

The following discussion covers some of the potential problem areas. While by no means complete, the topics listed may help you focus on the right questions. Normally, careful planning prior to a major presentation can flesh out the critical issues. Once you have anticipated the problem, you can devise appropriate solutions or safeguards prior to the solicitation.

The naming problem: Should the institution accept the "Adolf Hitler Chair in Modern European History"? The naming issue can provide a minefield of problems. Does the potential donor of the named building have an unsavory reputation? What will you say to the college's faculty, alumni, students, and friends when the donor for whom the new arts building is named is indicted a week after the dedication ceremony?

One law school named an endowed chair for a well-known attorney who had a reputation in the state as a bully who cut corners and could not be trusted. The chair was a substantial one, much needed by the law school, and the attorney had never been involved in any bar disciplinary procedures. The law school took the money and announced the gift with great fanfare. Instead of receiving acclaim and congratulations, the institution was deluged with criticism. Just the suggestion of wrong-doing on the part of the donor was enough to ruin the gift in the eyes of the public.

The anonymous gift problem: "Don't try to thank me." Whenever a donor asks that a gift be anonymous, your eyebrows should rise: How serious is he or she? Experienced fund raisers assume that every donor wants some form of recognition. Even if the donor sincerely wants to avoid public recognition, you should find an appropriate form of private acknowledgment.

Failing to fulfill the recognition expectations of a donor can have serious and long-lasting results. For example, if you accept at face value the donor's offhand request "not to make a fuss" and never offer any kind of acknowledgment, you are unlikely to receive anything more from that source. On the other hand, there are those rare cases where the donor really wants to be totally anonymous. In that case, you should be very careful to keep the secret. If the donor's name leaks out somehow, you may lose that friend forever.

It's very important that you have a complete understanding of the donor's true expectations and then respect those expectations to the letter. The converse can also be nettlesome, the donor who wants and expects far more acclaim than the gift warrants. If you do too much, you set a very burdensome precedent in the expectations you raise in other donors.

Making sure you really have a commitment: Fools rush in.... In the hurly-burly of a campaign, you may be tempted to interpret an oral promise of support as a firm commitment to give. Never announce a gift publicly until you are sure that you have one—with the commitment in writing. Imagine the embarrassment if you announce a potential but not yet fully committed gift. Or suppose that the not-yet-committed gift involves a naming problem. There may be public controversy that causes the embarrassed and angry prospect to withdraw the gift altogether. This story takes place in one form or another every year. And, unfortunately, the story is usually told in the headlines of the local press—a sure-fire way to ruin a major campaign, embarrass donors, faculty, staff, students, and the fund raisers involved.

Avoid this catastrophe by making sure you have a full commitment before an announcement is made. The general counsel at your institution can advise you on what is known as a "suable pledge"—one that you can enforce in court if it should come to that. He or she can also help you draft courteous, but legally adequate, letters of gift.

Restricted gifts: The ties that bind. How many strings are you going to let a donor tie onto a gift? If the donor restricts the use of the money to a certain purpose (and most donors do), how many restrictions can you accept? The fewer the restrictions, the more flexibility the institution has in using the gift. For example, it's much easier to fill a "Chair in History" than a "Chair in Medieval Spanish History with a Focus on the Inquisition."

The narrower the restriction, the more difficult it is to fulfill the terms of the gift. It is a tragedy today that so many institutions are saddled with unused and unusable endowments from gifts that were too narrowly restricted.

Frequently, the only way an institution can use an overly restricted gift is to go to court and use a complex procedure called the "cy pres doctrine." When granted, this doctrine permits the court to rewrite a gift restriction so that the funds can be used in a way that most closely meets the donor's original intent. This procedure is used in situations where, for one reason or another, it is impossible to comply with the donor's original language. A classic example would be a substantial gift to create scholarships for "white males." A court, through the cy pres doctrine, has the power to rewrite the gift to avoid serious questions of race or sex discrimination. But the use of cy pres is expensive, time-consuming, and uncertain. Believe me, you do not want to get involved in that process if you can avoid it.

Even more dangerous than the donor who wants to put too many restrictions on the gift is the one who wants to have a role in deciding who will receive the scholarship or who will be appointed to the endowed chair. This can also jeopardize the donor's tax deduction (check with a good tax lawyer before you proceed in this area) and will certainly offend the faculty members and administrators who would normally be involved in the designation process.

Faculty criticism: communication helps. Any dean knows that faculties are occasionally subject to bouts of unreasonable behavior, frequently resulting in a flood of criticism directed at a well-meaning dean. The area of fund raising is particularly subject to faculty outbursts. If you do not raise enough money you will be roasted. And, sometimes, you will be roasted even when you raise a major gift.

Sometimes when you announce a major gift to your faculty, expecting reactions of joy and acclaim, you may be surprised and dismayed to receive harsh criticism instead. They ask why you designated the chair to Zoology when everyone knows the next chair should have gone to Anthropology. Or they say, why did you ask for a scholarship when we all know that endowed chairs are what is needed?

Faculty members are notoriously naive about the prerogatives and interests of donors, with very little understanding of the fund-raising process or the problems it involves. Any major gift to one area of the institution may be bitterly resented by those in other areas. Jealousy is, it is said, the key to understanding all faculty politics. You will be accused of not consulting your colleagues. Anticipate this complaint by discussing these and other issues with your faculty colleagues before any major campaign. Educate the faculty about the realities of fund raising and the flexibility needed by the fund raiser. Leaving the faculty uninformed about this critical area of institutional effort may lead to faculty disputes and painful intercollege divisiveness.

Stewardship: Using gifts for the purpose given. It is absolutely critical that gifts restricted by the donor for a particular purpose be used only for that purpose—unless you have a court order directing otherwise. Borrowing money from one fund to support another area, whatever the justification and however pressing the need, not only exposes the institution to scalding public criticism, but also invites lawsuits and sometimes even criminal charges.

All institutions that receive gifts should have a well-defined stewardship process for restricted gifts. That process must include an administrative restriction of the gift to the appropriate use at the time it is received. Periodic auditing should take place to ensure that the donor's original intention is being fully respected. Improper stewardship—using gift funds for unauthorized purposes—if publicized, can destroy an institution's fund-raising potential for years. If the institution's alumni and friends do not believe their gift will be used for the purpose for which it was given, its gift-getting ability will be seriously damaged. (See Chapter 14 for more on stewardship.)

A sense of balance: Gifts that cost too much. How much should you spend to get a gift? What is the real net gain? Sometimes you pursue a donor for so long, and incur so many associated costs in the cultivation phase, that when you finally receive the gift you may well wonder if the gain was worth the cost.

We all know that you have to spend money to get money. You wouldn't launch a capital campaign without a budget big enough to do the job. Nevertheless, at appropriate points throughout any fund-raising endeavor, you have to measure your costs—not just in dollars but in time and energy as well—against the gain you hope to achieve.

Valuing the gift: The IRS, the donor, and you. Sometimes a donor may want an unrealistic valuation for a gift. The higher the value you can assign to a gift, the bigger the tax deduction—and the closer the IRS scrutiny of the gift. Valuing the gift is only a problem when you accept items other than money. Land, buildings, and valuable personal property such as paintings must all be valued, and, rest assured, the process by which you value these gifts will be subjected to careful scrutiny. Above all, you need to protect yourself and your institution from any suggestion that you have overvalued a gift in an attempt to aid a donor.

Screening devices

Screening devices, used both before and throughout the solicitation process, can help you avoid these and other ethical pitfalls. In a major capital campaign, for example, a coordinating committee should review all major gifts, and at least one member of this committee should be specifically designated to be on the watch for potential ethical pitfalls. Deans and faculty members engaged in fund-raising activities should attend regular training sessions that sensitize them to ethical issues. Some institutions require that all major proposals be reviewed by a separate office, such as the general counsel's office, where a trained person looks for potential ethical problems. Whatever screening mechanisms your institution uses, it is essential that there be some procedural device that forces fund raisers to think about these ethical questions.

Prospect research and privacy

The need for information on prospects can come into conflict with a prospect's right to privacy. We need to give considerably more thought to questions about appropriate limits to prospect research. At the beginning of a campaign, professional fund raisers usually arrange information-gathering meetings with alumni in specific geographical areas. The alumni are asked to chat about their fellow graduates, particularly those with substantial resources.

So far, that activity appears both essential to the fund-raising effort and harmless. No fund raising can succeed without reliable information that will enable fund raisers to tailor proposals to the particular interests and known giving abilities of prospective donors.

Nevertheless, there is always the danger that attempts to obtain personal information about prospective donors can cross the line of taste and permissibility, however ill-defined that line is. Where do you go to get the information you need? How do you deal with private and personal background information that the prospect would not want made public? With whom do you share information in the campaign? How do you safeguard sensitive information you obtain? Do you purchase information from others? Do you sell information to others?

All of these questions are just beginning to be discussed seriously by successful academic fund raisers. We need to give a great deal more attention to what is appropriate and what isn't in the sensitive area of gathering information about our institutions' prospects.

A return to the right mindset

One last word about attitude: Fund raising can be fun; indeed, it can be one of the most enjoyable aspects of a dean's or faculty member's job. To begin the task with that mindset remains important, despite the potential ethical pitfalls discussed above. The more fund raising you do, the more you will understand the innumerable ways you are helping not just your institution, but also the donor. A donor's lasting gift will affect generations of students and faculty. That donor, in a very real sense, is purchasing a form of immortality. He or she is playing a vital role in transmitting the values of higher education from one generation to the next.

If you have the right mindset, you will not find it difficult to ask a person of means for the money to achieve the mutual goal of serving higher education. It is not hyperbole to suggest that we are providing the donor with the priceless opportunity to be involved in one of society's most important tasks, the improvement of higher education.

A donor's attitudes about his or her wealth often depend on how that wealth was acquired. For example, it is much easier to talk to someone who has achieved third- or fourth-generation wealth—whose family has been actively associated with philanthropic endeavors—than it is to approach a self-made man or woman. The person who has fought and scraped for financial means may find it harder to part with some of it than the man or woman who was born into a wealthy family with a long-standing tradition of philanthropy.

The general background of most of your donors will depend on the type of institution with which you are connected. An Ivy League institution deals with many families that have enjoyed generations of wealth, while the donors to a new institution may be the first in their families to acquire the means to give. You will need to adapt your approach and cultivation techniques to the type of prospects at your own institution.

Conclusion

While it is true that "money talks," you need to give careful thought to what it is that the money is saying and at what point you need to talk back. The task of fund raising is challenging, satisfying, and enormously worthwhile. However, it can also be fraught with danger, filled with ethical pitfalls, and you have to be careful that you don't find yourself singing, "I wish I had never seen your face," to the donor who brought you big trouble with the big gift. Thus, while money talks, there are limits to what you can allow it to say. And when it says the wrong thing, it's time for you to say, "Thanks but no thanks."

Chapter 8

New Dean—
New Opportunities:
A Case Study

T he "changing of the guard" at an institution's top levels is too often a time of prolonged pause and planning. The new president or dean, especially if entering from the outside, feels compelled to study intricately the workings of the school, the patterns of giving, and the expectations from within and without. Unfortunately, inaction can slow the momentum of fund raising, blur the image of the school, and weaken the new leader's eventual standing with the school's support community. Certainly the new dean's or president's first acts should not be foolhardy. But when he or she realizes that there is no master plan that will make support cultivation a science, the new administrator can begin turning the problems of transition into opportunities for new approaches.

Turning problems into opportunities

Paul Rizzo arrived in 1987 as the new dean of the Kenan-Flagler Business School at the University of North Carolina at Chapel Hill with little idea of his expected role. Rizzo came out of business as former vice chairman of the board of IBM. He was a long-time supporter of the school, yet with minimal real knowledge of its inner workings. He knew personally many of its major contributors, but had limited experience sitting on the opposite side of the table and soliciting funds. What Rizzo did understand was the dangers of trying to know everything before doing anything. It became quickly apparent to observers that someone of Rizzo's composition had little temptation to remain inactive.

Among the first steps Rizzo and his development staff took was to go back to those who had so heavily recruited him and ask them to put their money where the praise had been. The goal was $125,000 of working money for what were called the "Dean's Initiatives." Those who had told Rizzo what a boon he could be for the school were asked to help give his incumbency quick momentum. He could not know yet exactly how he needed to spend the funds, so he needed them unfettered by conditions. He wanted total flexibility in appropriating them as his knowledge of immediate needs increased. Instead of apologizing for uncertainty, Rizzo promoted it as opportunity.

Not all gave, but enough did. If nothing else, this provided data for the new dean on who gave and who was just talking.

Rizzo also hit the road in a year-long tour of alumni organizations. The build-up to his arrival could not be allowed to deflate with a period of invisibility. Often a private luncheon with key local alumni would precede a much larger reception. What Rizzo heard at these gatherings was more important than what he said. People tell a new dean with a relatively open agenda a great deal more than they tell one touting a studied master plan. "My advice to academic deans is to get out and find out why people don't give money," Rizzo says. "It's pretty educational."

Public relations as a vital component

Hiring a public relations firm can be a public relations event in itself. At Kenan-Flagler, Rizzo had a number of goals in mind when he brought in outside help to evaluate the current status and potential of the school's communications efforts.

First, the act itself emphasized the way the school valued its alliance with the external public. News media covered the story. The message began to get out that the business school truly cared about its relations with the world around it. That message was important for supporters—people whose giving was often linked to the prospects of increased visibility. A school conscious of promoting its merits will also promote its benefactors.

Second, the public relations firm energized the faculty. Teachers began to see what they were doing through the eyes of the outside world. The firm went through the various components of the school asking what each did and how better to inform the public of the work. A public institution is accountable to its taxpayers and donors, faculty members were reminded. Besides, it is in the interest of the school (and the faculty) to increase awareness of its work.

Rizzo also organized an external affairs office. The office evolved to handle all major gift and annual fund giving, media relations, and marketing. Creating the positions and hiring the staff for this new office solidified the view that this was not a one-time event. Public relations was integral to all the efforts of the school and required constant attention.

Empowering faculty and staff for fund raising

Partly by necessity, partly by choice, Rizzo geared the faculty to run itself and to be responsible for a great deal of its own fund raising. He knew he had a very good faculty with very good degree programs. But they seemed to need empowering to manage their own programs. When he arrived, there was often limited funding for research. Yet, as with many schools, the business school's reputation waxed or waned according to the quality of the research being produced.

"The research agenda is important to the faculty," Rizzo explains, "because it keeps them up to speed with what's going on and gives them material to use in the classroom. It's important to fund raising, too, because we don't have a lot to sell if we can't sell the intellectual content of the faculty. The only way we can demonstrate that is with what they produce."

Rizzo had inherited a new building that housed the Kenan Institute of Private Enterprise. Its concept, to bring the academic and business worlds together, had yet to take full form. Working with the faculty and staff advisers, Rizzo began to flesh out the mechanisms for making the Institute work. One of the most meaningful moves in terms of the faculty was to establish "centers" for research within the Kenan Institute. These centers organize research efforts around particular sets of topics such as management studies or competitiveness and employment growth. Each center, run by constituent faculty, is responsible for collecting interested businesses as members. Members help fund research efforts and share in the results. Members also increase their familiarity with the school and its quality faculty and students. Faculty have a peer-managed source of research funding and improved access to business insiders.

According to Rizzo, the Kenan Institute has done more than any single program to keep the business school in the public eye. That exposure helps with student and faculty recruitment, which helps with the national reputation, which helps with fund raising. "It's like a chain," he says. "You start losing one of those things and the whole thing will fall apart." The faculty has grown to appreciate its role as a vital link and participates in keeping that link strong.

The dean's got to do it

A particular peeve for Rizzo is constant suggestions to form committees of major givers to assist in development campaigns. Others may have had success with that approach and encourage it, but Rizzo believes otherwise. No matter how supportive of the school and how well-respected they are, outside people "are not going to raise the money for you. The dean's got to do it," Rizzo emphasizes. "That's the message: The dean's got to do it."

That philosophy does not exclude major donors and supporters from playing a significant role in the overall efforts of the school. Soon after arriving, Rizzo formed a board of visitors. The goal is to get active business people in influential positions to understand what the school does. They are asked for money, for placement assistance with students, and for advice on school curriculum relative to other business schools and the needs in business. They are not, however, a development committee. If they do not choose to give money, that is acceptable. Because they are the right people, just having their names associated with the school helps with fund raising. They may help with access to other donors, with cultivation, but the asking must be done by the dean and his staff.

Rizzo's first year, besides the initial "Dean's Initiatives" campaign, was particularly concentrated on developing relationships. The relationships paid off. When the university-wide Bicentennial Campaign began in 1989, the business school added to the momentum with its own announcement of a lead gift of $10 million. In the process, the school gained a new name—the Kenan-Flagler Business School. Its public visibility was at an all-time high. This and other events led to the establishment of a new tenor for the school, one less associated with transition and more with success.

Capitilizing on momentum—learning when to shift gears

Serendipity always plays a significant role in success. Capitalizing on good fortune, however, is entirely in the hands of the leaders.

When a *Business Week* survey of the nation's top business schools came out for the first time, Rizzo had barely finished his first year as dean. No one at Kenan-Flagler expected much from the results, given the difficulty of measuring the relative worth of business schools and the seemingly unassailable position of some of the country's top private universities. The final tally, however, placed UNC eighth—above such schools as Stanford, Columbia, Chicago, and Duke.

The new dean was now associated with success. Rizzo knew better than to claim all the credit. Besides serendipity, there were all the school's attributes he had inherited. But taking advantage of the results was entirely his to claim.

"People don't give you money because you need it," Rizzo says. "They give you money because they think you're going to do something good with it and bring some distinction upon them." The *Business Week* rating worked perfectly into that philosophy. Rizzo and his development staff were able to cash in on the relationships they had been developing. They had listened well enough to suggestions from the early days now to answer concerns with clear proposals and proof of the school's worth. Rizzo made a point of challenging the level of giving of many of the school's regular supporters.

"When you're calling on influential people who drive nice cars and have great big offices and you ask them for $500, it's kind of a waste of your time and theirs," says Rizzo. "So you ask for lots of money and sometimes they say 'yes.' But sending out letters for annual gifts is the easy way out."

The giving for the school went from about $675,000 a year to more than $7 million. Engendering that kind of rise involves no magic. It takes hard, conscientious work on developing relationships and knowing when to ask for the money. Rizzo warns that giving needs to be managed so it is in line with the goals of the school.

Getting a lump of money for something the school does not want to do benefits no one. He also advises against thinking of businesses as a cornucopia of funds. "Individuals give much more than corporations."

The dean as inspiration, not perspiration

As Paul Rizzo retires from the Kenan-Flagler Business School after five years of service, he is proud of the reputation and development of the school. However, he would be the first to say that his role was far more one of inspiring than of doing. He managed a system where faculty and staff largely led themselves, where good advice from within and without the school was plentiful, and where opportunities presented themselves as much as they were created. What Rizzo did do was know how to capitalize on what was given.

"Unless you have something that's worth promoting, publicizing, and selling, it doesn't make a lot of sense to put a lot of money and effort in some big public relations and advertising budget," Rizzo emphasizes. No other school or institution can model its plans exactly on those at Kenan-Flagler because the givens will not be the same. What other organizations can learn from the Kenan-Flagler and Rizzo example is the need to take advantage of whatever situation they face.

Far from being at a disadvantage, a new dean—or any new leader—can find new opportunities in transition. There need be no significant sequestering period. Indeed, a vital public relations plan is crucial to gaining momentum and keeping it going. Fund raising is only possible when the dean takes the lead in providing visibility for the organization. The people and available skills a new dean inherits can be substantial, but they will only serve the organization when empowered to do so. Once all these efforts are made, capitalizing on new events seems inevitable.

Section 3

Continuing the Process to Completion

Chapter 9

Major Individual Gifts

Bronson C. Davis
Vice Chancellor for University Advancement
Texas Christian University

O ne of the first discoveries deans new to fund raising make is that the inclination toward philanthropy does not distribute itself equally among the population. Whether gift-giving is a learned behavior or a gene located somewhere in the heart, it quickly becomes obvious that it is a quality sadly lacking even in some of our best citizens. And when deans do find those splendid givers with grand records of philanthropy, and they make the perfect solicitation for a project they believe to be absolutely compelling, there will sometimes follow the inexplicable negative response.

Happily, the fund-raising vineyards contain a good number of charitable people who do say "yes" to our proposals. Trying to find these people, involve them, and get them to invest in our programs is the essence of the gift-making process. It is a process that most believe to be more art than science, but there are certain accepted presumptions and methodologies that guide most fund raisers. They are the grist of this chapter.

Many of us fall into the trap of focusing so intently on the needs of our programs that we forget that a match must take place in the gift process between our needs and the needs of our donors to express themselves philanthropically. It is only appropriate, then, that we begin with a discussion of what factors motivate individuals to become donors, and how our programs are structured to meet needs and encourage giving. For simplification, these factors are divided into "altruistic" and "self-serving" categories.

Altruistic factors that motivate giving

There is a sense in which Thomas Hobbes was right when he wrote, "No man giveth but with intentions of good to himself, because the gift is voluntary; and of all voluntary acts the object to every man is his own pleasure." Perhaps there is no such thing as pure altruism; even the most generous donor is satisfying psychological needs when he or she gives time and money to our enterprises. Nevertheless, the factors discussed below seem more altruistic than others.

• *Institutional loyalty:* Some people find meaning in life primarily through their commitment to an organization, whether it be a church, a college, a corporation, the army, and so on. These people have a strong sense of institutional allegiance. They are prime volunteers, the soldiers of our alumni associations and annual funds.

• *Gratitude:* Some donors give out of simple thankfulness for what the institution has done for them. Professors change lives, student activities provide vocational direction, living units produce lifelong relationships. The four years of college are a transforming time in people's lives, and for this experience many are grateful.

• *Spiritual beliefs:* Some donors give to a college or university because it is associated with a particular religious denomination, and giving is part of supporting their beliefs. Others give out of a combination of gratitude and a kind of providential insurance that their good fortune will either begin or continue. As Proverbs 11:25 says, "Be generous and you will be prosperous. Help others and you will be helped."

• *Responsibility:* People give because they feel a sense of responsibility for the welfare of particular organizations. John D. Rockefeller was the exemplar of this motivation, and it is the essence of stewardship: "I believe that every right implies a responsibility; every opportunity, an obligation; every possession, a duty." Albert Einstein made a similar point: "It is every man's obligation to put back into the world at least the equivalent of what he takes out of it."

• *Project orientation:* These donors are determined to accomplish something specific with their gifts. They seek to cure cancer, to improve the teaching of mathematics, or to build a winning football team. They want to see and touch the results of their philanthropy.

• *Desire to memorialize or honor:* These people seek to memorialize or honor someone and to perpetuate that person's memory and contributions by naming a chair, lectureship, or building for him or her.

Self-serving factors

Although fund raisers don't talk about these factors much publicly (except for taxes), these are among the factors they focus on when they are building strategies for major gift solicitations.

• *Recognition:* Nearly all people like to be recognized and thanked for the good they do. It is a fund-raising truism that we thank in as many ways as we can and as often as we dare.

• *Power:* Being able to give is a demonstration of a person's success in the world. As Erich Fromm wrote, "Giving is the highest expression of potency."

• *Guilt:* This is the flip side of responsibility. Fund raisers emphasize that you must do your fair share. You must pull your load if you are going to be on the team

Preliminary donor lists are sent out before the close of the year to shame those who "feel" they must be among the givers.

• *Leverage:* Fund raisers consider this factor primarily when they are deciding who should call on a prospect. The referring internist is chosen to call on the surgeon, the big publisher is selected to call on the printer, the corporate client calls on the lawyer. Some of the same thinking goes into choosing a fund-raising chair. Who has a lot of chits to call in?

• *Taxes:* The old saw was that taxes affected the timing and sometimes the structure of gifts, but not much else about giving. Initial analyses of giving in the 1980s, however, have shown that lower taxes have proved to be a disincentive to giving among large donors. The higher the cost of giving, the less giving. At the same time, including appreciated gifts as a tax preference item in figuring alternative minimum taxes threw much uncertainty and many complications into major gift fund raising. Thus, fund raisers are paying much more attention to tax policy as the impact of such policies on giving becomes clearer.

• *Immortality:* This is complementary to the desire to memorialize or honor someone. Donors seek a kind of immortality through gifts designed to name scholarships, chairs, and buildings for themselves. James Michener wrote, "The man who gives an adequate gift to a well-equipped American college is more sure of an earthly immortality than any other private citizen."

This is a reductionist view of the fundamentals of gift giving. At its heart, philanthropy is a business of human values and relationships. Nevertheless, any gift reflects a mixture of motives, with one or two of those mentioned above as dominant. The successful fund-raising organization will seek to uncover the possible motivations behind a potential gift and suggest ways in which the donor may satisfy particular needs. Both the donor and the organization benefit through this mutual exchange.

Fund-raising organizations strive to develop formal programs to satisfy many of the needs described above. Colleges and universities have formal gift acknowledgment procedures to thank donors for gifts of varying levels. Stewardship programs are designed to provide regular reports on endowed funds and the people who hold the scholarships and the chairs. Annual reports are published to recognize donors, and donor societies exist to make donors feel an important part of the educational enterprise. Special opportunities are marketed to provide vehicles for making commemorative and memorial gifts.

Fears of giving

In the late 1970s, another way of looking at motivational issues in fund raising was presented by Kerry McClanahan in a paper on "The Psychology of Donor Motivation," delivered at the Council for Advancement and Support of Education Summer Institute for Fund Raising in July 1977. McClanahan talked about the four fears of giving that fund raisers are likely to encounter:

• *Fear of loss and the surrendering of power:* In making a gift, a donor gives up control of part of his or her resources, exchanging a tangible asset for an intangible one. When a particular donor has a problem with this aspect of giving, the fund raiser needs to recognize the loss, but show the donor that the benefits of giving the gift, such as increased esteem or self-fulfillment, outweigh the loss. By giving, the donor becomes part of something greater than the individual self.

• *Fear of negative identification:* People do not want to be associated with negative outcomes or failing organizations. It is not a good sign when too many of your donors want to give anonymously. People like to associate themselves with positive, successful ventures, and so it is important for fund raisers to position their organizations in as positive a light as possible. A fund raiser cannot change the nature of the organization, but wherever possible he or she should emphasize the positive. If your institution is not doing "world class" research, then you need to emphasize its strong teaching or services provided to society. In most instances, the worst case for giving and the least effective is that the institution won't survive without the resources.

• *Fear of being forgotten:* Some prospects "love the courtship, but are impossible to get to the altar." Prospects who are subject to the "all you want is my money" syndrome fear that once the gift is made the giver will be forgotten. "Post-purchase dissonance" applies to gift-giving too! For this reason, some fund raisers keep people on the mailing list after they have made a gift. In fact, the most successful fund-raising organizations believe that cultivation doesn't really begin until the gift is made. Thereafter the donor receives a steady stream of birthday and holiday remembrances, invitations to special events, regular visits, and annual reports about the gift if it is endowed.

• *Fear of embarrassment:* Some donors like to set the pace, but others do not wish to appear to be too far in front of their peers in terms of giving. This is particularly true with younger donors. Others do not give because they fear their gift will be too small. And the "never" donors fear that their first gift will draw attention to the fact that they have not been giving. Fund raisers use various techniques to counteract these fears. They may discuss average gifts for classes and use gift tables to show how many gifts are required at various levels to make the final goal so that donors can find the appropriate niche. Gift reports showing levels of giving assist donors in giving gifts appropriate to their status. And for "never" givers, fund raisers can provide a dramatic illustration of the impact of their negative decision by multiplying the average alumni gift by the number of "never" givers.

The gift-giving life cycle

Another way to approach the gift process is to develop different mixes of programming for different stages of life. At Texas Christian University, we have developed information and education programs to help our students understand the importance of philanthropy in not only subsidizing higher education, but also in providing qualitative differences in their education and on the campus where they live and study. Students are part of TCU's telemarketing program, and they act as hosts and helpers to the alumni program. During their senior year, they are asked to make their first financial commitments through a senior gifts program.

Young alumni are our most valuable admission interviewers, and they have the discretionary time to be the organizers of the alumni chapter programs. They are also active in reunion programs and are suitable targets for insurance programs. Nevertheless, the first 10 years of life after graduation are also somewhat difficult for alumni directors and reunion fund raisers because young alumni often become quite self-absorbed as they start their careers and families.

Once alumni enter middle age, the possibilities increase for meaningful involvement and gift-giving. We try to enroll as many as possible in the $1,000 annual fund gift society, and we begin the cultivation process for those with major gift potential. Reunions become even more significant, and involvement in key volunteer slots is important.

When alumni reach the age of 45, we start sending them planned giving materials designed to help with educational, retirement, and estate planning. This continues throughout the rest of the life cycle in the hope that the alumnus might provide a bequest to endow his or her annual gift. Once beyond educating the children, donors enter their prime earning years and generally give their largest gifts. The vast majority of the large major and leadership gifts comes from this group. The 25th through 50th reunions become key opportunities for gift-giving and cultivation. And it is toward the end of their lives that those with strong philanthropic instincts usually choose to make definitive gifts.

The gift continuum and the involvement cycle

Figure 9-1 shows another way to view the life cycle approach. The gift continuum graphically illustrates the winnowing process that is critical to successful fundraising organizations. Fund raisers like to say that every gift is important, but, in fact, large gifts play such a predominant role (in comprehensive campaigns it is not uncommon for 90 percent of the money to come from 5 percent or fewer of the donors) that to be effective, good programs must be able to identify and grow their leadership donors. Fund raising is basically an elitist enterprise in which the only requirement for participation is the capacity to give.

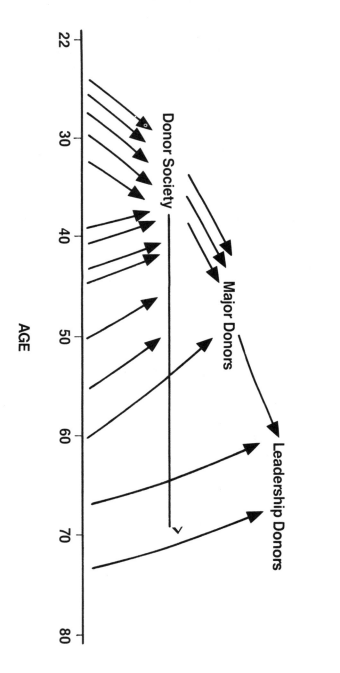

Figure 9-1

No discussion of the gift process would be complete without covering the involvement cycle. This was introduced by one of the pioneers of fund raising, Harold "Si" Seymour; elaborated on by another important figure, Buck Smith, long-time development chief at the College of Wooster and former president of Chapman College; and made famous by David Dunlop, director of capital projects at Cornell University. Figure 9-2 demonstrates the five steps in the development of major gift prospects:

- identifying the prospect;
- providing the prospect with information:
- developing the prospect's interest in the organization or institution through involvement; and
- getting the gift investment.

Figure 9-2

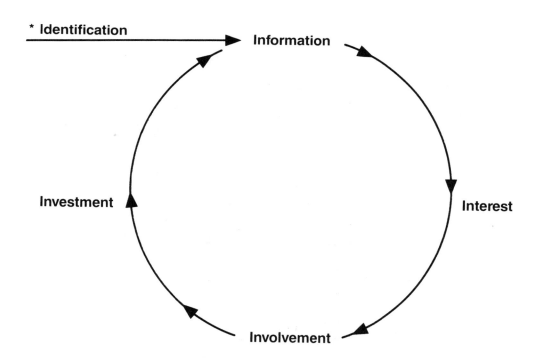

Every college and university has a story about a previously unknown individual who died and left $1 million to the institution. But for every one of these there are 99 who were painstakingly nurtured through the years and finally were inspired to make that principal gift.

Involving prospects in the ongoing life of the institution is the key to successful major gift fund raising. It is sometimes difficult for deans to understand why "outsiders" should be brought within the walls of the academy, but it must happen if a fund-raising program is to provide the needed resources. That is why volunteer opportunities as trustees or service on visiting committees, donor society boards, planning committees, and in executive-in-residence programs are so important. Prospects who feel part of the ongoing life of the school see the importance of their gifts and are ever so much more willing to invest.

The extension of the involvement cycle into a cyclone-like illustration by David Dunlop (Figure 9-3) provides an even more meaningful characterization of the gift process. The good organization is continually trying to cycle and recycle donors to keep them interested in the institution.

Figure 9-3

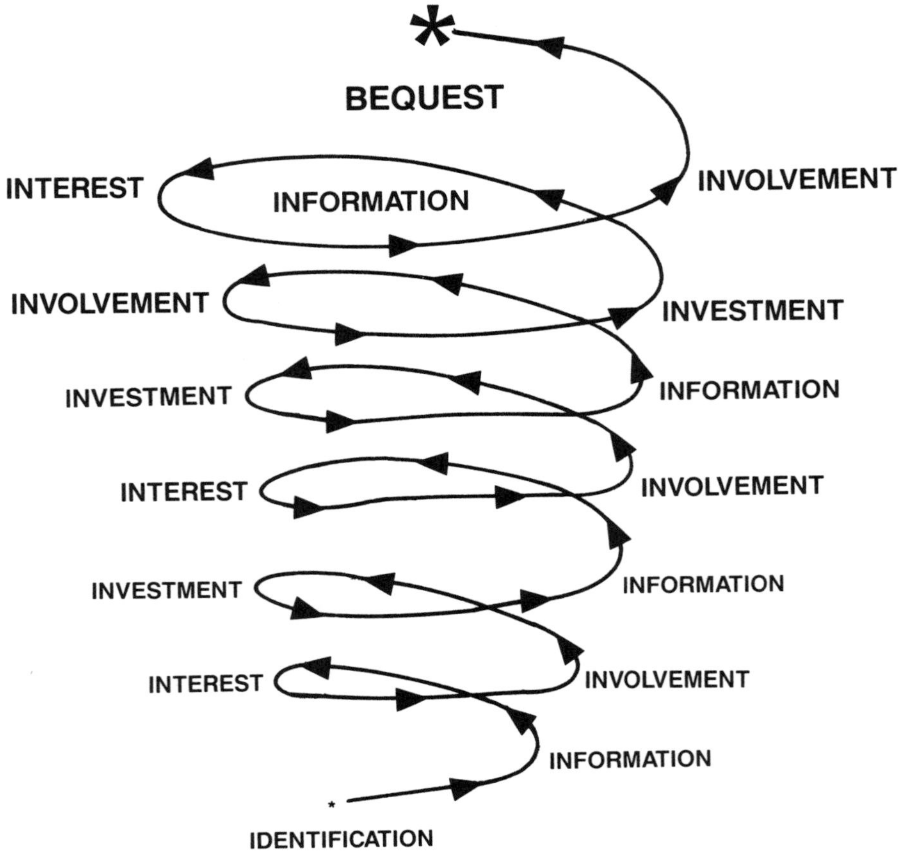

BEQUEST

INTEREST — INFORMATION — INVOLVEMENT

INVOLVEMENT — INVESTMENT

INVESTMENT — INFORMATION

INTEREST — INVOLVEMENT

INVESTMENT — INFORMATION

INTEREST — INVOLVEMENT

INFORMATION

IDENTIFICATION

Figure 9-3 also illustrates a second important concept in major gift fund raising—positioning. Many major donors already have carefully planned giving programs. In order to turn a prospect into a new donor, the fund raiser has to make a case strong enough either to get the donor to increase his or her giving or to shift giving priorities. Every request must compete with requests from other worthwhile organizations, and the fund raiser strives to establish a favorable position for the institution. This is a process that must go on continually. A fund-raising organization that allows a donor to drift or lie fallow faces the risk of seeing that gift diminish or disappear.

Those are some of the primary concepts involved in major individual fund raising. It is the richest and most rewarding area of development activity because it involves people giving expression to their highest aspirations, which, in turn, produces wonderful results within the institution. Most development officers spend years in the field before they become major gift officers, but deans begin their fund-raising careers at this point. And for many it may well be the best part of their deanship.

Chapter 10

Corporate and Foundation Gifts

Mary Kay Murphy
Associate Vice President for Development
Oglethorpe University

One of the greatest philanthropists of our era, Robert W. Woodruff, had a motto that we can apply as we build our fund-raising team from among the institution's deans, faculty, and development officers: "There is no limit to what can be accomplished so long as no one cares who gets the credit."

As a dean or faculty member—in a decentralized research university, a centralized multi-college university, or a small liberal arts college—your success ratio will be higher if you consider the following as you prepare to raise funds from corporations and foundations:

1. *People give money to people they know and trust.* Corporate and foundation donors are no different from individual donors in that they want to know and trust those in the institutions that receive their gifts and grants. Working with the development office, you will be a member of a team that creates strategies for key college university representatives to get to know corporate and foundation decision makers and to create with them relationships built on trust. The most successful solicitations will be built on relationships that several of your team members have with corporate and foundation donors.

2. *When a proposal is made, it will have its best chance for success if it follows an existing relationship built on trust and if it provides benefits to both parties—the grant maker and the grant seeker.* The larger the request, the more important that a series of meetings and discussions precede the submission of a proposal. Especially with corporations, but also with foundations, the proposal must address the needs and interests of the grant maker.

3. *Peer solicitation—individuals of equal status, power, and rank participating in an exchange that benefits both—is the strategy that produces the best results*

in fund raising. Ideally, a trustee representing your institution will ask a corporate or foundation peer for an institutional grant or gift. Other times, the president's relationship will be that on which a corporate or foundation request is based. There might be times when your relationship with a corporate or foundation leader will be the key. Close work with the development office will help determine the best approach for peer solicitation of corporations and foundations. Your role will be very important as these strategies are developed, whether or not you are the primary contact or are part of the formal solicitation call. The most successful solicitation will come from the right person asking the right person for the right amount at the right time—with no one caring who gets the credit.

4. *Development officers do not set the priorities for college or university fund raising.* Grant makers insist that before requests are considered the college or university attest to the priority allotted to the project within the institution. Is it the top priority? If not, what is? Is there a formal planning process in place to identify priorities? If not, why not? How long until such a plan will be in place? To determine these priorities, you as a dean or faculty member with others of your colleagues will be part of a team that identifies institutional priorities. The plan may take different forms, depending on your institution's readiness for private fund raising—the traditional accreditation plan, a long-range plan, or, best of all, an institutional strategic plan. (See Chapter One, "Setting the Table for Development.")

5. *Although being an advocate for your department or college is one of your most important responsibilities, your program is but one of many in your college or university.* When there are competing priorities in the institution vying for corporate and foundation support, it will be the role of the president ("The Buck Stops There") to make a final decision about which program to approve for external funding requests. It will be best if his or her decision is based on an institutional strategic plan. Corporations and foundations will insist on this internal process, especially in the unfortunate circumstance of your institution seeking funds for two or more competing projects from the same corporation or foundation.

6. *Before committing to a plan for raising private funds, get to know the odds of success for your strategies.* Only 5 percent of total philanthropy traditionally comes from corporations and another 5 percent from foundations. Individuals contribute by far the most money to philanthropic causes. In 1991, for example, of the $124 billion total philanthropic contributions, nearly 90 percent came from individuals, almost 5 percent from corporations, and a little over 5 percent from foundations. However, for higher education a different contributions profile emerged. Of the $10.8 billion contributed to higher education in 1991, 26 percent came from alumni, 23 percent from nonalumni individuals, 22 percent from corporations, and 20 percent from foundations. Nine percent came from religious and other organizations. These percentages have remained constant with slight variation over many years. You should know these data and consider them as you put forth strategies for corporate and foundation fund raising.

7. *Your institution's chances for success with corporate and foundation fund raising will improve after careful analysis of sources for private support.* Which corporations or foundations are closest to your college or university—in terms of

location, prior support, and product or program related to your curriculum? Which have alumni or faculty connections? Which have previously utilized campus programs such as continuing education, library resources, fine and performing arts activities, and contract research? Build a strategy that relies on support from local, regional, and national corporations and foundations that have had or could have relationships linked to your program.

8. *Your institution's success in fund raising will relate directly to your attitudes about asking for money from corporations and foundations.* How do you view fund raising? In a positive light? In a negative frame of reference? A little of each? You as a dean or a faculty member have a positive role to play in bringing potential donors to worthy causes for support. Your university's current and future faculty members will benefit from your commitment to becoming a member of a successful fund-raising team. Only in the United States of America is corporate and foundation fund raising institutionalized in the way and to the extent that it is. Philanthropy—the joy of giving—benefits the donor as well as the cause. The more you share a role in this activity, the more positive your view is likely to be about being a fund raiser and about the benefits of fund raising.

9. *Your institution's success in fund raising will also relate directly to your attitudes about working with the development office.* Do you think the only professionals in the college or university are faculty members? Do you view fund raising as a necessary but distasteful human activity? Do you know about the help and benefits the development office can give you with corporate and foundation fund raising and other types of fund raising as well? It will be important for you to be honest with yourself about your perceptions in regard to the development office if a successful team is to be built, if the university is to have success in fund raising, and if corporate and foundation donors are going to find in your university priorities in which they want to invest.

10. *The most effective role you as a dean or faculty member can play is in building relationships with corporate and foundation decision makers.* Corporate employers of graduates from your program will want to know you. Ties that you have to your university's alumni working in corporations or linked with foundations will help build on those relationships. Your leadership in your profession—law, engineering, medicine, mathematics, political science, music—will provide you with entree into some corporate and foundation grant areas. Your college or university will benefit from your reputation as a leader in your professional associations and disciplines. Your sensitivity in building these extended relationships and advancing your college or university as you do so will be key to building bridges within your institution for success in corporate and foundation fund raising.

After reviewing these general issues, you as a dean or a faculty member will want to consider three additional areas in corporate and foundation fund raising:

- trends in corporate and foundation support in the 1990s;
- strategies for attracting support; and
- role delineation for deans, faculty, and development officers in building bridges with corporate and foundation donors.

Trends in corporate and foundation gifts in the 1990s

In the strategic plan that you as dean are building for your academic program, there will be reasons to seek corporate and foundation grants. Corporations produce equipment that your faculty and students need. Foundations are required by law—as individuals are not—to give away a portion of their assets. A corporate or foundation gift can lend prestige, recognition, and leverage as you seek gifts from individuals, including alumni, community members, and friends. These gifts also provide leverage with other corporate and foundation requests.

The economics and demographics of the 1990s are having a direct impact on college and university fund raisers who seek grants from corporations and foundations. One of the most visible trends is the shift among these sectors to support elementary and secondary education. As a dean or faculty member, you will need to be aware of this trend. Perhaps you will want to relate your project to this community need as you make the case for support of colleges and universities. Perhaps you will not want to consider any link of your project to a community need other than your own. Whichever way you lean, it is important for you to be aware of the corporate and foundation trend for support of elementary and secondary education, rather than higher education.

Another trend, but a related one, is increased competition from other community groups for philanthropic support. Issues related to the homeless, AIDS, child abuse, and battered women, for example, did not compete directly with support for higher education in the 1980s. Again, the economy and the demographics of the 1990s have produced a shift as increasingly important community issues compete with seemingly less urgent needs for support of colleges and universities.

Another trend of the 1990s is the increase in restrictions corporations and foundations are making on their grants to colleges and universities. These include refusal to support college or university overhead charges; requirements for greater accountability for uses of funds; limits on funds made available for only a portion of the project (called seed money grants); and requirements that one grant be made to several cooperating colleges or universities. Such consortia arrangements provide only a portion of program funding. This form of support is meant to provide leverage as the institutions seek other contributions from corporations, foundations, and individuals.

Strategies for attracting corporate and foundation support

With the emergence of such trends, you as a dean or faculty member will benefit from developing strategies for ways to successfully solicit corporations and foundations. Some of the strategies for you to consider include the following:

1. *Position your department or college.* Be aware of changes in demographics, environment, attitudes, needs, and trends among the general constituencies your department and college serves. These include current and future students, current and future parents of your students, current and future employers of your

graduates, and leaders in your community. Identify ways to move your program or college in concert with these changes or to anticipate the changes and be a leader in solving problems related to them.

2. *Coordinate internally.* Although your department or college is your highest priority, communicate with faculty, other deans, development officers, the president, and additional key players what your program and fund-raising plans are and how you want to proceed. Be mindful of clearance procedures on corporate and foundation prospects and follow them. Be a team player. If your program cannot be approved internally on this round, what can you do with the other team members to see if it can be approved next time? How can you be a useful advocate for your program and build bridges for its support with your college or university colleagues? Remember what Robert Woodruff said, "There is no limit to what can be accomplished so long as no one cares who gets the credit."

3. *Package "consortia" efforts.* In this day of corporate and foundation concern for getting the highest return on investments, "the biggest bang for the buck," work with other college or university deans and faculty members—on your campus, in your community, around the country—to determine how you might combine efforts, seek joint funding, and provide innovative solutions to problems of interest to corporations and foundations. Do not go too far in this planning process before you make contact with possible corporate and foundation funding sources. Involving these decision makers early and often will likely result in a better, more collaborative fund-raising approach.

4. *Commit to long-range or strategic planning.* Corporate and foundation decision makers want to know what prompted your request of them. Is it part of the college's or university's top priority list, or is this your idea of building a kingdom which does not relate to the college or university as a whole? Developing a strategic plan for your college or university should be one of your president's top priorities for action. It will be if your institution is preparing to enter a comprehensive fund-raising campaign and is serious about being successful with corporate, foundation, and individual donors. Strategic and long-range plans differ in that strategic plans take into account changes in the environment external to the college or university and relate these to budgets and investments of university revenues. Long-range plans do not create goals based on conditions external to the university such as age of the population, shifts in income by race and class, or other market-driven forces. Although you might benefit from a strategic plan for your department or college, the preferred approach will be for the institution as a whole to commit to a strategic plan. You will find this process and plan to be a vital asset as you prepare to seek corporate and foundation funds.

5. *Build a strong board of advocates.* Working with the development office, identify 10 or more key community, corporate, and foundation-affiliated leaders who will be asked to serve on a board of advocates for your department or college. These members should represent potential funding sources for your department or college—well-placed alumni, nonalumni individuals, corporate and foundation decision makers. If potential board members are not employed directly by potential sources of corporate or foundation support, it is a fair expectation that

they would have ties to funding sources and be willing to use these ties on behalf of your department or college. You will ask board members to support your program before they ask others to do so. Of course, the same holds true for you as a dean or a faculty member. Before you ask others to make their own contributions, you will want to declare your leadership and make a financial commitment to your program.

6. *Increase visibility through campus events, publications, and communications.* Separate chapters in this book provide extensive detail about the methods and techniques of increasing the visibility of your department or college through campus events, publications, and communications. The importance of identifying key corporate and foundation prospects and including them in these initiatives cannot be overstated. These will be key activities for you to undertake to get to know people in the corporate and foundation world and to help them to get to know and trust you, your program, and your university.

Role delineation for deans, faculty, and development officers

Building bridges with a team composed of you as a dean or a faculty member, members of the development office, and others including the president, trustees, and consultants is imperative for success in raising corporate and foundation funds. The multiplier effect will benefit you as you bring together the talents, skills, and perspectives of different members of your team. Centralization or decentralization of the fund-raising program will create different patterns of roles and responsibilities. Size of your institution will determine who on your team plays which roles. At this point, it is important to review the activities involved in seeking corporate and foundation support and to have you as dean or a faculty member determine how to apply these roles in your department, college, or institution.

1. *Setting academic priorities.* Only you as dean with your faculty can set academic priorities for your program. Once these are identified, the development office can help you to determine which corporate programs or which foundation priorities might relate in programs or priorities. The strength of your programs, not your need for funds, will be what will attract corporate and foundation support. Thus, plan from strength, not from weakness or need.

2. *Identifying and clearing prospects.* Working with your development office, create a list of corporate and foundation prospects and seek institutional permission—or clearance—to approach prospects for contributions and funding. Include in the list corporations and foundations with links to your curriculum; alumni with interests or contacts who could help; nonalumni who could help; vendors whom your program has supported; and likely others in the local, regional, and national or international networks you are working to build.

3. *Involving boards of advocates or advisers.* Seek assistance from members of your department's or college's advocate or advisory board. Ask them for names of their corporate and foundation contacts. Request clearance of these names from the development office. Include alumni and nonalumni individuals, especially com-

munity leaders and possible parents, who can help you create links and relationships with corporate and foundation donors.

4. *Targeting corporate and foundation sources for support.* After careful research on your part and with the development office, determine which types of requests will be appropriate for corporations and which for foundations.

Corporations are possible sources of support for research grants (a deliverable study or report), equipment, operating grants, program support, in-kind noncash gifts, and matching gifts.

Foundations are likely to be approached for support for challenge grants, program grants, research grants, scholarships (not for individuals), fellowships, young faculty development grants, building or renovation grants, equipment grants, and operating grants.

5. *Setting up solicitation meetings.* After cultivation events have taken place on campus and exploratory meetings have been held at corporate or foundation sites, it will be important to set up a meeting to make a formal solicitation. The prospect might signal the timing of this meeting after appropriate cultivation has taken place. At other times, it will be important for you and the development office to initiate these meetings with corporate and foundation decision makers. An average of 18 months to two years will likely take place between initial cultivation and final solicitation. Teams of presenters will be ideal, although, if warranted, as many as three from your institution might be included on the call. The composition of your team will depend on the corporation or foundation team being solicited. Peers need to solicit peers. If the call is on the chief executive officer, your president will need to make it, along with a representative from the development office or you as dean. If you as dean have the relationship with the prospect, your presence on the call will be key, perhaps with the president, a trustee, or a development officer. At times, faculty members will be part of the call. The project presentation should be invited or at least announced when the meeting is being scheduled. The visit should be cordial but brief. Benefits to the corporation or foundation should be identified and commented on as a major part of the presentation. Benefits to the university should be addressed, and the visit should end with a next step identified.

6. *Writing the proposal.* The proposal might be submitted following the solicitation meeting to confirm what was requested and discussed. It might be submitted, after cultivation has invited it, before the meeting takes place. It should follow the foundation's or the corporation's proposal format, if there is one. It should speak to the need for the program and the amount requested (the need relates to the institution's strengths and the community or corporate benefit, not the financial needs of the university), the objectives of the program or project, the methods for carrying out the program, the evaluation techniques that will be used to measure the program's success, and future funding sources for the program when corporate or foundation funding ends. Unless the proposal will be reviewed by a panel of scientific experts as in civil or electrical engineering or medicine, the proposal should be prepared by the development office. Familiarity with writing proposals for corporations and foundations will be a strength that members of the development office can provide to you as a dean or a faculty member.

7. Thanking the corporation and foundation donor and providing reports on results. Stewardship is the most important aspect of a successful corporate and foundation fund-raising program. Thanking the donor adequately and frequently, reporting on project results, recognition of the gift and of the donor—all are part of the vital activity of stewardship. Inviting the corporate or foundation representative to campus to observe the program or building funded will be an important part of sharing the vision for the university's future with those who have invested in it. Some foundations and corporations want publicity about the gift and attendant forms of recognition at special events, in university publications, and on dedicatory walls. Others will not. It is important that you as dean in concert with the development office clarify the donor's wishes and carry them out to the full extent of these directives. With some corporations and foundations, one gift will beget another. With others, the first gift will be the only gift. Stewardship is not meant to be manipulative in setting up an automatic next gift. Rather, all activities related to stewardship of a gift are meant to thank the donor and to be accountable in reporting on the uses of the gift and the benefits to the corporation or foundation as well as benefits to the college or university.

Corporate and foundation support, in summary, can best be achieved by a team of deans, faculty members, and development officers who subscribe to three tenets of successful fund raising:

1. People give money to people they know and trust.
2. There is no limit to what can be accomplished as long as no one cares who gets the credit.
3. The right person asking the right person for the right amount at the right time is the result of well-built fund-raising bridges linking deans, faculty, and development officers for results that benefit the college or university as a whole.

Chapter 11

Involving Faculty in Development

George H. Jones
Vice-President for Research and Graduate Studies
Dean of Graduate School of Arts and Sciences
Emory University

I t is almost a truism to say that the faculty of any academic institution have a significant stake in the development of that institution.

Faculty serve the institution as purveyors of knowledge and counsel to students and colleagues. Faculty are served by the institution as they derive benefits from the successes of the development efforts made for and by the institution. Nevertheless, the scope of the activities of the institution's development or advancement office may not always be obvious to faculty. Faculty may also be unclear about what the relationship should be between their individual interests and those of the institution and between their activities and those of the development office and its officers.

An institution that wishes to establish an agenda for faculty-related development activities must take several steps:

1. It must involve faculty in the process of setting institutional priorities.
2. It must articulate institutional priorities.
3. It must accommodate faculty entrepreneurship to institutional objectives.
4. It must connect faculty activities to faculty involvement in development.

Involving faculty in setting institutional priorities

Before the institution can involve the faculty—or any member of the college or university community—in development activities, it must have a well-conceived set of priorities and objectives, as well as mechanisms for assessing its progress toward meeting those objectives. In other words, effective development must be based on a clear and crystalline institutional vision. Essential elements of the development and maintenance of such a vision include long-range planning; setting specific objectives for individual schools, departments, and programs; and developing strategies to achieve those objectives.

If faculty are to be committed supporters of the development activities of the institution, they must be involved in setting the institution's priorities. Faculty support almost always requires faculty participation. Faculty Priorities Committees, appointed by the dean or provost, are an effective way to involve faculty in developing the institutional agenda. The involvement of faculty in this way does not abrogate the prerogatives of the institution's administration, but ensures that the faculty have a voice in determining direction for the institution.

Articulating institutional priorities

Once priorities have been proposed, they must be shared with and discussed by the community. This may seem obvious, but institutions do not always provide the forums and other opportunities in which the priorities, the mechanisms used to establish them, and the strategies envisioned to accomplish stated objectives can be discussed.

Faculty involvement in the advancement of the institution requires that there be channels for dissemination of any information that may be relevant to faculty interests, functions, and commitment. Meetings involving faculty, academic administrators, and advancement officers are an effective way to provide information and stimulate discussion of the institutional agenda. Such meetings may be held at the school or college level, at the level of department and program chairs and directors, and with individual department and program faculty. Appropriate campus publications should be used to publicize proposals relating to the institutional agenda. A clear articulation of proposed institutional priorities should attract the attention and stimulate the participation of faculty.

Accommodating faculty entrepreneurship to institutional objectives

Faculty members at any institution will have agendas that relate to their own professional and personal development. In many, perhaps most, cases, those agendas will be consistent with the more global objectives and priorities of the institution. In other cases, the attempts by faculty to accomplish their own legitimate professional objectives—that is, their ability to be successful entrepreneurs—may conflict with the more comprehensive aims and activities of departments, schools, or the college or university.

It is essential, therefore, that faculty be clear about the role of the development process and the development office in facilitating not only the achievement of institutional objectives, but also the professional objectives of individual faculty members. Faculty must understand that institutional priorities might sometimes take precedence over their own agendas. In return, the individual agendas of the faculty should be supported not only by the development enterprise but also by the academic hierarchy—the chair of the faculty member's department, the dean, and when necessary the provost and the president.

The establishment of the kinds of relationships suggested above does not mean that faculty entrepreneurship should be discouraged. On the contrary, the ability of individual faculty members to attract resources to support their own activities should be an essential component of the institution's overall development strategy. However the needs and interests of the individual faculty member must, in almost every case, be balanced with those of the institution. If there is conflict, the priorities of the institution are likely to take precedence. If faculty participate in the development of those institutional priorities, such decisions should occasion only minor difficulties.

Connecting faculty activities to faculty involvement in development

An important prerequisite to the involvement of faculty in development activities is a thorough understanding of what faculty *do,* that is what faculty themselves feel are their responsibilities to the institution. Faculty are involved in the creation and dissemination of knowledge—teaching and scholarship. Both teaching and scholarship contribute to the learning environment of an academic institution, and it is important to emphasize that students are not the only "learners" in that environment. Faculty scholarship contributes to the increase in human knowledge generally and to their own intellectual development.

What the foregoing analysis suggests is that faculty participation in institutional development requires more than an understanding and acceptance of institutional goals. It also requires an understanding of what faculty do and an appreciation of their contributions to the institution. Faculty participation in development is likely to be encouraged to the extent that the institution acknowledges and supports faculty activities.

The institution should recognize strong scholars and develop mechanisms to applaud not only those faculty whose accomplishments are sufficiently glamorous to attract attention from the outside world, but also faculty whose work, although solid and substantial, is not considered "newsworthy." Similarly the institution should recognize outstanding teachers and develop mechanisms to reward strong teachers—and not only those who may qualify for the Galactic Award for Teaching Excellence. The institution's development office can play a key role in helping schools and deans create programs that recognize the contributions of faculty. Faculty support of the activities of the institution's development office will be facilitated if that office in turn supports the activities and interests of the faculty.

It is important that the faculty understand that development means more than fund raising. Faculty may not realize that the development enterprise might include the institution's news and information service, its publications office, and its conference and meeting service. There is a clear connection between these subdivisions and the recognition of faculty contributions, which they can facilitate. Faculty need to understand that the development office can be a valuable contributor to faculty interests—assisting with student recruitment and retention, for example. Presentations by development staff at school, college, or departmental faculty meetings can clarify the role of the development office.

Involving faculty in development

Once the elements discussed above are in place—institutional priorities are set and articulated; mechanisms are established to ensure a faculty role in the shaping and refinement of the institutional vision; the relationship between faculty and institutional priorities is considered and a system is established to recognize faculty contributions to the institution—the institution needs to consider specific ways in which faculty can be direct participants in the development process:

1. *Faculty can participate in the planning of specific development initiatives.* In addition to their participation in setting institutional priorities, faculty have an important role to play in the planning and implementation of specific programs designed to meet the objectives that relate to those priorities. In particular, faculty input should be of considerable value in formulating fund-raising strategies for projects related to a particular discipline.

For example, if the institution is planning to build an arts center, faculty in the performing arts departments should be an excellent source of advice and counsel in planning how it will be funded. Similarly, the faculty in a particular discipline should be asked to help design a plan to fund an addition to the library collections in that discipline. This kind of faculty participation won't happen automatically. The development office needs to actively solicit faculty input throughout the planning process.

2. *Faculty can identify alumni who might become donors and supporters of the institution.* Faculty establish relationships with their students that frequently extend beyond graduation. Faculty can identify alumni who might be recruited to support the devleopment initiatives of the institution, and support is not confined to financial contributions. Institutions naturally expect many of the alumni to make financial contributions, but alumni also play an important role as emissaries, advocates, recruiters, and supporters in general of the institution's programs.

3. *Faculty can assist in the identification of potential corporate and foundation support for the institution.* Many faculty establish relationships with corporations and foundations in connection with their field of discipline. These relationships can be used to garner support from those agencies for larger institutional initiatives. For example, a faculty member in the chemistry department may have established a connection with a chemical company that may be willing to

help fund the new wing for the institution's chemistry building.

4. *Faculty can play a role in the cultivation of specific donors.* If a potential donor has interests that relate to a particular discipline, a faculty member in that field may be able to speak to those interests. The faculty member can outline specific needs of a program or project in the field and can also give the prospect a broader view of how the specific program would further the objectives of the institution.

5. *Faculty can enhance the visibility and the image of the institution.* Faculty can serve as ambassadors for the institution in the local community, with alumni clubs outside the local area, and with colleagues at other institutions. Many faculty travel to other colleges and universities to attend meetings and conferences or to do research in their field. The institution's development office can recruit these traveling faculty. For example, a trip to give a seminar or attend a meeting might be coupled with a speaking engagement at an alumni club. While the institution may need to provide some financial support for the extra travel this would entail, the potential return from this level of involvement by faculty will probably more than offset the cost to the institution.

6. *Faculty should be direct contributors to the institution's fund-raising programs.* In addition to the contributions faculty can make as advocates, ambassadors, sources of information, and so on, it is reasonable to expect that faculty will make their own financial contributions to the institution as well. Faculty who have a voice in creating and maintaining the institutional vision, whose teaching and scholarly contributions to the institution are recognized and valued, and who are committed to the continued advancement of the institution should be willing to add financial contributions to the others they make.

Chapter 12

Effective Calls and the Art of Asking

Shirley Anne Peppers
Director, West Coast Development
Harvard University

L ike almost everyone else, you probably get nervous when you must ask for money. Even though the funds are not for your personal use, you feel slightly embarrassed. This is not why you went into academia, and this is not how you want to spend your time. There is no guarantee of success, and it will be humiliating to be turned down.

These are the feelings most of us share when contemplating soliciting someone for money. You, however, have an advantage over many of us.

Most prospective donors admire the work faculty do. Faculty and deans are respected in our society, and alumni, friends, and parents are honored to have a chance to meet personally with a professor or an academic dean. Even when they disagree with an academic's ideas, they still regard faculty as highly intelligent and creative. They respect the choice most scholars have made to work in a noble, and underpaid, profession. Many academics have forgone lucrative careers in the private sector to pursue teaching and research, and donors are aware of this.

The work you do is important, not only to your students and the direct beneficiaries of your research, but to your institution and to society as a whole. When you chose an academic career, you did so, at least partly, because you admired faculty you worked and studied with when you were a student. You held them and their work in high esteem. Now students see you that way, and so do administrators, the professional fund raisers with whom you work, and, most assuredly, the prospective donors whom you meet.

When you ask a donor to support your program, department, or research unit, you are giving that donor several precious gifts: the chance to be a better person, the chance to participate in the work you do, and the chance to have a positive influence on the future.

When the donor agrees to your request, you will have accomplished two important goals: You will have helped to meet a major need of your institution, and you will have helped another human being reach a high level of self-actualization. By realizing that what you do is noble and that you are giving donors opportunities they would not otherwise have to achieve greatness and recognition for doing what they want to do, you can be reminded that you have every reason to approach donors with confidence and pride.

Your personal attitude about asking people to support a project, your department, or a whole division will be the single most important element in your success as a solicitor.

Developing your Case for Support

A fundamental and important part of preparing for a solicitation is making sure that you have a solid, important reason to ask for support. Working with your fund raiser, you can articulate the needs of your program, why it is important to meet those needs, how gifts will solve problems and meet goals, and how donors will be recognized for providing gifts in the ways you are asking.

A Case for Support is different from a proposal for a specific gift. As a prelude to a series of solicitations or to a campaign, it is important for you to develop a set of academic priorities and then to translate those priorities into specific needs and gift opportunities. This, incidentally, is one way fund raising helps with the core missions of our educational institutions: Because priorities must be defined for fund raising, the goals and objectives of the institution are reviewed, examined, adjusted, and renewed by the faculty and administration.

Thus, the core components of a Case for Support are why what you do is important and what it will take to continue, to grow, and to improve. Depending upon your circumstances, you may also need to address budget control and cost-cutting measures, as well as other means to ensure that your project, department, or school is getting the best value from every dollar spent.

A written case will help your cause. The length might vary from a few typewritten pages to a glossy 100-page brochure. The written case should articulate clearly your needs and gift opportunities. Not only will that help you early on in presolicitation meetings with donors, but it will help you to be sure you know what you need. Knowing what you need (and do not need) will help you direct donors' gifts to areas where they will be most helpful.

Where you can, delegate the actual writing of the case to a development officer or a staff writer. If you are fortunate enough to have a fund raiser who works on behalf of your area, be sure to use him or her as much as you can, not only for developing and writing the case, but in every aspect of your fund-raising efforts.

The right prospective donor

Deciding whether someone is a good prospective donor is not as easy as it sounds. Particularly for the largest gifts, the top few gifts that can create or fundamentally alter a program, donors typically have had a long and evolving relationship with the program or institution. That someone is wealthy and lives in your community does not make him or her a good prospect for your cause.

Your sincere interest in the people who may support your project is a prerequisite for developing the long-term relationships that will lead to gifts at endowment levels. Again, development officers can help you identify prospects and can do much of the work necessary to encourage the associations that lead to gifts. It is not necessary or even desirable that you attend every meeting or event. Let your fund raiser help decide when your personal action or presence is required. Your involvement should be special.

Donors of large gifts have usually made smaller gifts along the way and gradually have increased their levels of giving and involvement. However, it is important to pay attention to new donors, parents of current and past students, and friends of deeply involved donors.

Past supporters are the best source of future donors. They already are committed to your work and have a vested interest in its continuance and success. They will make gifts in the future. They are your best fund raisers. Their advocacy on behalf of your program or school will be very convincing to other prospective donors. Therefore, not only is it right and reasonable to be grateful, and to demonstrate your gratitude, but it is in your program's interest that you devote some time and energy to continuing the relationships you already have.

Locating prospects is not the subject of this chapter, but some attention to analyzing and extending your prospect base should be a fundamental part of your development program. Sustained effort in this area will be very fruitful over time.

Developing a solicitation strategy

If your prospect has a relationship with your program—if your fund raiser or other staff have kept in touch with the donor, invited him or her to occasional events, provided regular updates on how a student fellowship is being used, and thanked the donor properly for all past support—figuring out a strategy should not be too difficult. Unfortunately, sometimes one has not developed the perfect relationship that flows naturally into a major gift.

There is no formula for devising successful strategies. There are, however, some steps that will increase the possibility of a positive response to your request. First, ask yourself a few questions:

• Who should ask for the gift? Review with your fund raiser all the possible solicitors, and determine who has the best likelihood of receiving a favorable hearing.

• Does the donor have philanthropic intent? Your donor must want to make a gift.

• Is the donor ready to be asked: Has he or she been involved in meaningful ways?

What kinds of involvement has he or she had? Over what period of time?

- Does the donor understand and support your needs?
- Can the donor make the kind of gift you plan to request? What evidence do you have of his or her capability?
- When should the prospect be solicited? What is there about his or her life that makes now a good time? Your needs are important, but the prospect's own situation will determine whether you receive support. Look at it from the donor's point of view.
- Both from your perspective and from the donor's, what needs to happen before the actual solicitation? Is a proposal necessary and/or ready? Has the president agreed to your idea of a building devoted to Medieval Studies, for example?
- Who generally participates in the donor's decisions to support your program? An accountant? Spouse? How should these people be involved?
- Under what circumstances have previous gifts been made?

Getting an appointment

The secret to getting an appointment is asking for an appointment. The tough part is getting yourself or someone else to make the phone call—especially when you are nervous about the reason for your visit. Fortunately, as a dean or faculty member, it will not always be necessary for you to place the phone call. One of the ways development officers can be of tremendous help is by setting up these meetings for you.

There will be a few cases where you must telephone personally. However, most of the time, it will be more efficient for someone else to call. Also, deans, faculty, and department heads are tremendously busy, and when you insist on doing this part yourself, you frequently become a bottleneck. Only for your few largest potential donors might it be necessary for you to telephone. In a phone call where some development expertise will be helpful and some explanation about the purpose of the appointment may be required, a development officer can make the call for you. In other cases, where the donor should be expecting to see you for a solicitation, your secretary can set up the appointment.

Whoever makes the call should be prepared to explain the purpose of the visit, who will be coming in addition to you (maybe a volunteer or a fund raiser), and how long the visit will last. During the conversation to set up the appointment, whoever makes the call should know and be able to articulate the reason for the visit.

It is important that the donor know you are coming to ask for a gift. Surprise is not helpful in this situation. At the meeting, you want the donor to have given some thought to your needs and to be open to listening to your proposal.

The donor solicitation meeting

This section covers the "donor solicitation meeting" as though all the stages were included in one session. Usually, it takes several meetings to go through all of these stages. Some of these appointments will be handled by staff, some by volunteer peers of the donor who support your program at high levels, and some by development officers, planned giving officers, or other campus experts in real estate, estate planning, and endowment management.

There are many ways to dissect a donor solicitation meeting. I like to think of four steps:

1. Listening for the donor's interest and readiness.
2. Questioning the donor to reconfirm his or her specific interests and goals.
3. Asking the donor for the gift.
4. Listening for the donor's response.

Some parts of the donor meeting/interview are very obvious, but when we are nervous, the obvious sometimes gets left out. It is useful, even if you are very experienced, to review the basics before each important meeting.

Thanking the donor for seeing you and for his or her past support should be one of the first things you do once the serious part of the meeting begins. Since you will know the donor and he or she will have some history with you, there may be some general conversation before the meeting really gets under way.

This early part is important and should not be rushed. The donor may be as nervous and apprehensive as you are. After all, if the donor has been properly prepared, he or she may soon have to consider one of the most important gifts of a lifetime. Easing the tension and reestablishing rapport will help the rest of the meeting be productive and satisfying to both of you.

Listening and questioning. Listening and questioning are intertwined during the conversation, and you should be doing most of the listening right now. At this stage, the donor should already understand your needs, at least in a general way. While you will have to make a specific request for support later in the conversation, you hope the donor will do most of the talking here and you will do most of the listening. And by listening I do not mean merely waiting for a pause in the conversation so you can make your next point, but active, engaged listening for what the donor is saying, not saying, and implying.

Your questions and comments should be related to the reason for your visit and open-ended, such as:

* How do you feel about the way your scholarship is working?
* Tell me about your visit to the faculty symposium last month.
* How did you feel about the students you met last time you were on campus?
* How did you react to the president's address to the board of trustees last week when she presented the list of academic priorities?

During this part of the conversation, the donor may raise objections that you will need to respond to in a frank, thoughtful, and caring way. Even when you feel he or she is wrong, it will be important for you to acknowledge the objection, recognize how an intelligent person could have that opinion, and then react to the specific statement. First, however, be sure you know what the objection really is.

An objection to admissions policies may really mask disappointment that your institution rejected a beloved grandchild or niece. The donor may be angry or disappointed at the response (or lack of one) he or she received to inquiries about the status of the granddaughter's application. Instead of recognizing the donor's relationship with the institution by some special treatment, the admissions office ignored the donor's concerns. (I am not implying that the rejection was improper, just that the way it was communicated is important.)

An objection to the work junior faculty are doing may mask hurt feelings at not receiving an invitation to a special lecture in the department or not receiving a thank-you note for a luncheon the donor hosted on behalf of a faculty member.

Another time, an objection may be based on misinformation. Then, you can either correct it on the spot or take steps to ensure that the donor gets the right information. Of course, a donor's objection may be valid or unanswerable, and then you will have to acknowledge that fact.

The objections of the advisers are as important to answer as those of the donor. That the donor values their opinions is evident by their presence. Sometimes they are speaking for the donor who is reluctant to raise an issue or does not feel competent to ask certain technical questions.

If a trust or other planned or deferred gift will fund the program, or if a gift of real estate is being contemplated, it is important that you include in one of the early visits to the donor someone who is knowledgeable in these areas. Frequently, these questions are crucial to the ultimate decision, and the donor (or his or her advisers) may be unwilling to go forward until these issues are addressed.

Depending on the donor's interests and what you intend to ask him or her to support, these kinds of questions should give you confirmation of, or cause you to reassess, your evaluation of the donor's readiness to consider a solicitation.

Asking for the gift. Asking the donor for the gift is the most difficult part of the solicitation process for most people. Many scholars just do not feel they can solicit someone for money. However, if you do not ask, you will not receive. Once you have covered the preliminary steps and the donor is willing to hear your request, someone must ask for the gift. Who should make this request should be given much consideration as it is probably the single most important factor in determining success. Sometimes it may be you, but it may also be a staff member, a volunteer donor, the president, or someone else whom the donor respects.

While there are no magic words, a gift is not likely to come your way unless you ask for it. There are two specific actions that someone must take to encourage the result you want:

- Someone must ask for the gift.
- That ask must include a specific figure or gift range.

Here are some sample words you can use:

- "Mrs. Smith, will you consider a gift in the range of $100,000 to $250,000 to support faculty research?"
- "Mr. Brownley, I know how much your scholarship meant to you when you were a student. Will you contribute $20,000 a year for five years to endow a $100,000

undergraduate scholarship at our college?"

• "Mr. and Mrs. MacAlister, your leadership and support of this campaign would get us started on the right path. Many others will consider our requests more seriously if you join us at this early stage. Will you consider a leadership gift of $5 million to name the new Humanities Complex?"

None of these asks would occur in a vacuum. In the sequence appropriate to each, you would have discussed the donor's interests, you might have presented a written proposal, and you or someone else would have agreed to solicit the donor. The "ask" does not suddenly appear out of nowhere.

Listening for the response. Listening for the donor's response is the next step, and it is a crucial one. Often, there is a period of silence after the direct request is finally made, and that silence usually feels very awkward. Most people are tempted to rush in to fill the void and proceed to undermine the request they have so carefully led up to and made. Because of nervousness, they begin to backpeddle.

Wait for the donor's response. Allow the donor the courtesy of answering your question. While you are not likely to get an immediate "yes," you should let the donor take the lead. You should also be prepared to accept graciously whatever response the donor makes.

At this point, you and your colleagues should be ready to answer questions, talk more specifically about the request, and suggest follow-up steps. Follow-up steps might include drafting a letter of intent for the donor's review, meeting with the donor's financial advisers to begin to work out how a large gift might be funded, arranging a follow-up meeting to respond to the donor's questions and objections, or setting a time to present your recognition ideas.

If you have led up to this point carefully and sensitively, the donor's response should be some variation on "yes" or "I'll think about it." However, if it is "no," your response should be just as gracious as if it had been "yes." Ask some open-ended questions. Now or later, ask what you should have done differently. Try to find out why the donor turned down your request. Also, a rejection of your request for the time being is not a rejection of you personally. And remember, often that initial "no" is the first step toward a "yes."

Conclusion

Finding the resources to carry on your important work, that of your laboratory or department, and that of other faculty and students has become almost as important as the work itself. Most faculty and deans want to spend only the time necessary to do it well because your lives are full of other demanding obligations and opportunities. Making use of your staff resources, developing a sound case for support, approaching the right donors with thoughtful strategies, and asking for specific gifts will help you move toward success.

Chapter 13

Major Gift Fund Raising: The Process at Work

Robert L. Virgil
Dean
John M. Olin School of Business
Executive Vice Chancellor for University Relations
Washington University

M ajor gifts play a critical role in achieving the long-term goals of any institution, particularly when those goals are pointed toward making quantum advances in the quality of the institution's programs, people, and prestige. Having an ambitious, yet well-defined and feasible plan for institutional progress creates a natural framework in which the major gift development process can take place.

Commission on the Future

In the mid-1970s, when I became dean of the business school at Washington University in St. Louis, the university was poised to undertake the Commission on the Future of Washington University, the most comprehensive self-study in its history. At that time, the university's business school was underendowed, highly dependent on tuition income, and not recognized as one of the nation's best schools; its new dean was also fairly new to academic administration and un-schooled in the ways of fund raising. The school then occupied cramped quarters—a converted dormitory, ill-suited for the school's mission of service through teaching and research. It had a very small community of benefactors with a history of interest in capital projects and few avenues for engaging alumni and other potential donors in the life of the school.

The Commission on the Future comprised 10 task forces, each representing a major division of the university. The task forces were made up of trustees, alumni, and other community and professional leaders. The Business Task Force included national and regional executives and leading business and economic educators. During 1980 and 1981, the task force conducted a spirited study and analysis of the key issues facing the school; it then presented several major recommendations about the school's objectives and priorities.

Under an umbrella overall recommendation—"that having a nationally recognized business school be a top priority of Washington University for the 1980s; and that Washington University vigorously support the development of the resources needed immediately and longer term to attain this objective"—the task force identified three specific steps to be taken:

- construction of new facilities;
- strengthening of the faculty and its research capabilities; and
- improvement in the academic programs, particularly at the graduate level.

The members also recognized that the school's previous pattern of growth by increments would not work, and that the goal of having a top business school could not be accomplished without the highest degree of commitment by those both inside and outside the institution. The recommendations of the Business Task Force became a vision or constitution for the school's advancement and the road map for its participation in a university-wide campaign, the ALLIANCE FOR WASHINGTON UNIVERSITY. That campaign sought to achieve many of the recommendations that arose from the deliberations of the 10 task forces of the Commission on the Future of Washington University..

The ALLIANCE campaign

The school's most urgent and critical needs were addressed through the highly successful ALLIANCE campaign, which ended December 31, 1987. With the help of a dedicated development team, a committed volunteer organization, and strong leadership from the university administration, we built and equipped a state-of-the-art, $14 million facility for business education. We acquired the business school's first endowed scholarships, five in all (we have since added four more). The school's endowment surpassed $50 million and is projected to reach $60 million by the end of 1992—from a base of $400,000 in 1978. We greatly expanded resources for student financial aid for both BSBA and MBA students with a popular sponsored scholarship program. We strengthened existing programs and introduced new ones of high quality and distinctive character. We greatly increased alumni participation and levels of support through planned events, new communications vehicles, recognition programs, and expanded opportunities for alumni involvement.

Perhaps of greatest consequence, through the task force and subsequent efforts to involve alumni and friends, we developed a core of committed individuals who understand the school, support its aims, and set an example for others by their work on its behalf.

A cornerstone gift names the school

The most significant outcome of the school's success in the university campaign was the announcement in January 1988 of the largest commitment in the business school's history—a $15 million grant from the John M. Olin Foundation for endowment and for naming the school in honor of the late John M. Olin, a leading industrialist and philanthropist who had served on the university's board of trustees for 40 years. This cornerstone gift owed much to Olin's long-time interest in Washington University and the established relationship between the foundation and other university divisions. The grant, the largest ever made by the foundation, was presented as a challenge fund to be earned by the school through matching contributions of new endowment and increased annual support over a five-year period to end December 31, 1992.

The sequence of events from 1980 to 1992 has had an indelible impact on development efforts. The Business Task Force has given the school new direction toward lofty but attainable goals, as well as a core of informed and involved volunteers. The ALLIANCE FOR WASHINGTON UNIVERSITY campaign and the John M. Olin Challenge provided the school and its supporters with the stimulus of operating in "campaign mode," the ideal setting for fund raising, for a dozen years. This environment, combined with the strong commitment of the university's leadership and the school's external constituencies to its goals, has enabled us to raise our sights, focus our efforts, and sustain our energy as we put in place a well-conceived program of major gift development. Our supporters have responded enthusiastically to the opportunity to share in doing something important for the business school.

The dean's role: Building relationships

Washington University is structured as a composite of academic divisions linked by a central administrative unit that provides general services, including staffing and support for development, alumni relations, and public relations activities. Each academic unit is responsible for raising its own revenues and managing its own expenses. The dean is not only the school's chief academic officer and budget manager, but also its chief fund raiser.

The role of the dean, along with fellow faculty and the development staff, in building relationships with potential donors is key to the school's total development program. This is especially true in the context of a major gift program, where a donor wants and often needs to work with the dean, department chair, or program director on a personal, one-to-one basis to direct a commitment and define its purpose. Attention to relationship building demands and deserves a significant commitment of the dean's time and energy.

The John M. Olin School of Business, by its nature, has concentrated great efforts on building relationships with the corporate community; it is a given that a business school must interact on many levels with those who practice what it teaches. However, the identification, cultivation, and solicitation of individual major gift prospects has also been extremely important in sustaining the momentum of the school's steady advances toward its long-range goals.

The major gift process does not begin and end finitely; it is a continuous flow of activities and gestures, of action and reaction. Nor can the development activities designed to secure the big gifts be isolated from other aspects of the development program. Indeed, it is invariably the opposite. Major gifts often result from an alumni reunion gift effort or planned giving program or as an outgrowth of involvement in annual giving programs that offer the satisfaction of personal contact between donor and recipient, such as sponsorship of student scholarships or faculty fellowships.

Those who have already made major commitments continue to be top prospects. We have an excellent example of that. The donor who gave us a seven-figure gift to establish the business school's first endowed professorship in 1981 followed through a couple of years later with a significantly larger amount to name our new building.

Case studies: Friends and donors

In the nearly dozen years since the Business Task Force recommended a set of high goals for the business school—goals that it believed could be attained if the school's supporters could be motivated and mobilized—the John M. Olin School has earned consistently generous support from corporations and foundations. However, the school would not be where it is today without the generosity of individual alumni and friends who have been partners in the school's continued progress. The following examples show how a relationship has developed between the school and three major donors.

Mr. and Mrs. A. Although Mr. A was a graduate of the business school in the 1920s, he and his wife had not had a long-term record of supporting the school. It was not until his 45th class reunion that he announced a gift, through a bargain sale of stock, of nearly $170,000 to establish an endowed scholarship fund as a memorial to his parents. He subsequently increased the fund with an additional gift of more than $20,000 in honor of his 50th reunion.

The A's were identified as prospects for the school for the ALLIANCE campaign and subsequently made two pledges (a total of $800,000) toward the new building. The gifts were used to name one of the most widely used public areas.

My first contact with Mr. A came when the director of development arranged a lunch for the two of us to meet him during the planning phase of the campaign. We determined that Mr. A had both the interest in the school and the capacity to make a major gift. Also, importantly, we all became friends.

We invited the A's to school and university events, including a dinner to meet the recipients of their scholarships. They invited us to their home and to important family affairs such as wedding anniversaries. The friendship we developed continues to this day. Mr. A also became involved as a volunteer. He was invited to serve on the school's capital resources committee for the campaign. He also served as a volunteer on our major annual giving society's membership committee. Because of Mr. A's interest in his class reunions, he was asked first to serve as his class's bequest and trust agent, then as class gift chair for his 60th reunion. Since her husband's recent death, Mrs. A remains keenly interested in the school's progress.

Mrs. S. The wife and daughter-in-law of St. Louis business executives, Mrs. S first began a relationship with the university when she and her husband established a fellowship fund in the medical school. After her husband's death, she established an endowed business scholarship in his name and followed that with an endowed fund in the business school library in her father-in-law's name. With additional gifts, her support to the business school now totals more than $500,000, to the university nearly $1 million.

Mrs. S had for several years been a member of the Women's Society of Washington University, an organization that provides services for students. As she became involved in the business school's progress through the campaign, although not an alumna, she volunteered at phonathons, built personal relationships with the students receiving the scholarships that she sponsored, and has become a confidante and trusted friend. She was recently awarded the Dean's Medal for her many contributions to the Olin School.

Mr. and Mrs. M. Mr. M is a late 1940s graduate of the school. He and his wife came to their current level of involvement in the school through their interest in alumni programs and activities, varsity athletics, and student recruitment. Mr. and Mrs. M have participated in the alumni travel program, travel lecture series, and in many other alumni programs. He has been a member of the school and university alumni organizations and a volunteer for the annual giving clubs. The couple began sponsoring an annual scholarship in the late 1970s for a business student involved in varsity sports; a little more than a year later, they established a writing award for business freshmen.

Mr. and Mrs. M have subsequently made two major gifts that reflect their involvement with faculty and students. The first was a $75,000 commitment to name a faculty lounge in the new building. Then, on the occasion of Mr. M's 40th class reunion, they made a pledge to establish an endowed fund to perpetuate the scholarship gift they had been making on an annual basis. The couple remain heavily involved in alumni activities and interested in the business school's and the university's progress.

As in the other two cases mentioned, the M's developed personal friendships with me, my director of development, and others at the university. One of their first scholarship recipients was a basketball player. The M's began attending his games and now, several years later, faithfully attend every football and basketball game at the university.

Teamwork is essential

In each of these cases, I played a pivotal role as dean in helping develop and expand the relationship between these people and the school. However, it would be unrealistic to imagine that one administrator can sustain the level of contact necessary for effective cultivation and solicitation of major prospects and stewardship for major donors. It takes teamwork by staff, including school development officers, planned giving and major gift officers, corporate and foundation relations staff, among others. It also takes a network of involved and loyal volunteers, which in itself demands a commitment of time and energy to develop.

At the John M. Olin School of Business at Washington University, we now have the structures and resources in place to attract prospects to the school and involve them in its activities and advancement. These include the Business Alumni Association and its related committees, annual giving clubs and programs, lecture series, Distinguished Business Alumni Awards, Excellence in Business Awards, the Dean's Medal, scholarship dinners, expanded reunion activities, school publications and newsletters, and others. We provide appropriate recognition for our donors, we express our appreciation, and we maintain regular contact on a personal level.

Building a major gift program takes patience and perseverance, time, energy, teamwork, and support from others. The rewards in accomplishment, satisfaction, and friendship far outweigh any statistical achievement in fund raising.

Section 4

Other Considerations

Chapter 14

The Importance of Stewardship

Donald G. Myers
Assistant Dean for Development and Alumni Relations
University of Pennsylvania Law School

One of the first lessons we are taught as children is to say "thank you." As fund raisers we sometimes forget this valuable lesson—to our regret. Nowhere is saying thank you with youthful appreciation and sincere gratitude as important as in academic fund raising. For it is well-known that past donors who have been properly thanked are every institution's best prospects for future gifts. (In this chapter, I use the term "institution" to include academic departments as well as colleges and universities.) This process of thanking and acknowledging donors is known as stewardship.

Thanking donors is not only the nicest part of academic fund raising, but it is also—second to "asking"—the most important. Good stewardship is an essential component of a sound development program. Stewardship responsibility includes:

• ensuring that resources are being used to the fullest extent for the purpose the donor intended;

• being sure that the intentions of the donor are being carried out fully;

• involving students, faculty, and administrators in expressing thanks and appreciation;

• encouraging repeat gifts from informed donors;

• making new friends with relatives and associates of donors and with others in the community who observe the institution's stewardship; and

• confirming the institution's reputation for good management, integrity, responsibility, and caring.

Organization of stewardship

In order to gain the rewards of stewardship, the stewardship function must be well organized, and the key to accomplishing this is the individual chosen for this reponsibility. If you, as dean, are that person, you will need excellent organizational skills and the ability to ensure that there is one outline of goals to follow and that appropriate steps are being taken to accomplish these goals. You will need to establish an area where donor files are stored. These files should include all correspondence and information about the donors:

- donor's full name, business and home address, and business and home telephone number;
- spouse's and children's full names;
- donor's and other family members' affiliation with the institution;
- all educational institutions the donor, spouse, and their children have attended; and
- the purpose of the gift and how it is being used.

Components of the stewardship process

The stewardship process involves three components: recognizing the motivation of the donor; acknowledging the gift; and preparing for the next gift request.

The first step is to recognize what motivates donors in order to make an appropriate acknowledgment. Among the main motivations of donors are to help others and to contribute to solving a problem that interests them. Donors want their gifts to make a difference, and the institution should use the acknowledgment process to reinforce the significance of the gift and to make the donors feel that they are more than just a funding source for the institution.

The thank-you letter

The institution's letter should demonstrate that the gift is truly appreciated and that the person who has given it is worthy of special attention.

Research. Before starting to write, ask yourself these questions:

1. What is the donor's relationship with the institution?
2. Does the donor know the person who will be signing the letter?
3. Has the donor given to the institution before? If so, when, how much, and for what purposes?
4. Why is the donor making this gift now?
5. If the gift is in honor or memory of someone, who is that person? Usually that individual is linked to the institution in some way.
6. What do you know about the program or project the donor's gift is supporting?

Opening paragraph. The opening paragraph should do two things: It should extend thanks, and it should convey that the writer knows something about the gift—who it's from; what it is (outright contribution, pledge, pledge payment, gift in memory or honor of someone); and what it's for. Some examples of opening paragraphs follow:

> It was a pleasure to learn of the latest payment on your pledge to the [building name] project. Thank you so much for your continued support.

> Thank you for your generous contribution to the John Smith Fellowship Fund at the School of Arts and Sciences. It is thoughtful of you to make this gift in memory of your husband, and we are most appreciative.

> I am writing to express my gratitude for the wonderful commitment that Handy Products has made to the institution to establish the Handy Products Professorship in Material Sciences.

> I have just learned of the gift you made to the [project name] this spring in honor of your parents' 50th wedding anniversary. Please accept my thanks for your kindness. It was certainly thoughtful of you to mark such a special occasion by your donation in your parents' names.

Body of the letter. Having made it clear in the first paragraph that the institution knows who the donor is, what the gift is, and what it's for, you can use the body of the letter to do the following:

• Comment on the gift: Tell the donor why the gift is important. Try to imagine what making this gift means to the donor and respond to that impulse, as in the example below:

> John Smith was one of the institution's most distinguished alumni, and we are both proud and honored to have a chair in his name here. By strengthening our ability to attract outstanding individuals to our faculty and to keep them there, the John Smith Professorship will do much to ensure the high quality of teaching and research at the Law School. You have chosen a splendid way to honor your husband's contributions to the practice of law and his ties to the University. All of us are grateful for your generosity and thoughtfulness.

• Sometimes you will have nothing to say about a particular gift. For example, if this is the 50th payment that Mrs. Smith is making on her pledge to the Smith Chair, you have probably said all you have to say about what the professorship and Mr. Smith mean to the institution. When this happens, you can praise the donor:

Building up the institution's endowment for faculty support remains one of our foremost goals. It is good to know that we can count on your steadfast support as we strive to achieve this end. You have been a wonderful friend to the Law School, and we are in your debt for all that you continue to do to help us.

- If you have nothing to say about the gift or the donor, touch on a recent or forthcoming event at your institution, as in the following:

The [Nth] Commencement ceremonies were held on May 16 and attended by some 20,000 people. As always, it was a wonderful celebration, and we were fortunate in having lovely weather. I am enclosing a copy of Jane Jones' keynote address. I am sure you will find it as inspiring as we did.

- If nothing remarkable comes to mind, suggest a visit to the institution:

I know Florida is a long way from [institution's location], but I hope you'll think about paying us a visit sometime. Perhaps we could get together next spring if you decide to attend your 45th reunion. I will give you a call within the next few weeks to see what we can arrange.

Closing. Reiterate gratitude for the donor's generosity:
- "My thanks again for your generous gift. Your concern for the [project's name] well-being is warmly appreciated."
- "It is encouraging to see the work of our institution supported with such generosity and enthusiasm. Many, many thanks."
- "We will always be grateful for the generous commitment that you have made to keeping the institution a vital and thriving place."

Other forms of acknowledgment

Although the letter is the quickest and least expensive form of acknowledgment, other innovative forms of appreciation add a greater personal touch and may be more appreciated by the donor such as:
- a face-to-face thank you;
- a small gift, such as a potted plant or t-shirt;
- a telephone call when a gift of a significant amount is received;
- letters from students explaining how the gift benefited their educational experience at your institution.

Reports to donors

Not only should you acknowledge the gift promptly, but the institution should periodically report to the donor, family, friends, and other interested parties about how the gift is helping the institution. Reporting to donors keeps them focused on the institution and what it is accomplishing.

Following are the different stewardship responses to the three major types of gifts—annual gifts, capital gifts, and endowed funds:

Annual giving. Annual giving donors should receive a brief report that provides details on the funds' uses, their value to the institution, and the continuing need for annual fund contributions.

Capital gifts. Reports should be made to donors who have made capital gifts for the construction or renovation of buildings. They should receive at least one progress report while the work is going on and another when the project is completed. You should invite donors to the dedication or open house. If they have been promised plaques in recognition of their support, be sure these plaques are in place by the time of the dedication.

Once the building project is completed, donors should continue to receive information about it. Invite them to events in the building and keep them posted on the building's impact on educational programs.

Whatever the purpose of a capital gift, the donor should receive a report. For example, a donor who has contributed to a standing program should receive a summary of the program's accomplishments a year after he or she made the initial gift.

Endowed funds. Reports should be made to donors who have endowed funds that support professorships, lectureships, scholarships, fellowships, research, prizes, building maintenance, and the like. Since endowments are the gifts that keep on giving, you should send periodic reports that explain how the funds benefited the institution and those who received them. If an individual is receiving the fund, the report to the donor should include a short biography of the person, mentioning his or her undergraduate institution and degree, work experience, and topic of thesis, dissertation, or research.

Securing repeat gifts

Good acknowledgments and reporting are not only a basic responsibility of the fund-raising operation; they are also one of the best ways to secure repeat gifts. Gift recognition is part of the cultivation for the next gift. If the donors feel that they have been properly recognized and are pleased with the institution's handling of their gift, they will be more likely to give in the future and to encourage others to give. This is a critical aspect of successful academic fund raising.

Central to good stewardship is that gifts are used in the way the donors intended, with scrupulous attention being paid to the donors' wishes. Before the institution embarks on any public donor recognition ceremony, it should gain approval from the donors to use their names publicly. Some donors may want to remain anonymous, and the institution must respect that wish.

Volunteers

Although the majority of donors give money, don't forget those who give their time—volunteers. They provide a valuable source of help, experience, and new insight, and the institution couldn't get along without them. Here are some ideas for thanking volunteers:

- Make a master list of volunteers' birthdays and send them a birthday card.
- Give a small gift related to the institution around the holidays.
- Create certificates of appreciation for volunteer chairs.
- Have a party at the end of the year, project, term in office, and the like.

Just as pleased past prospects encourage others to give, pleased volunteers encourage others to volunteer.

Conclusion

Good stewardship involves understanding donor motivation, creating a form of acknowledgment, and preparing for the next ask. The strong influence of good stewardship on donors' attitudes toward the institution and the results of these favorable attitudes should make it a priority in fund raising. Stewardship fulfills the institution's responsibility, illustrates its integrity, and encourages repeated gift giving. Stewardship is more than just an acknowledgment letter; it is a key to successful academic fund raising.

Note

The majority of this information is based on Benoit, Jean; Bush, Leslie; Hunt-Johnson, Nora; and Ray, Brit, *Donor Relations Handbook: Development and University Relations at the University of Pennsylvania,* Philadelphia, 1989. The handbook is a working document prepared by the staff of our donor relations department and is used as a desk reference by development officers campuswide. The text of the thank-you letter comes directly from samples provided in the handbook and the spirit of the "theory" is also drawn from the handbook.

Further research and support were provided by Tammara Flax.

Chapter 15

The Dean's Role
in Smaller Institutions

William R. Lowery
Vice President for External Relations
Carleton College

A s the sole officer in charge of academic affairs at a small institution—
say, a liberal arts college—you may inhabit a world substantially different
from that where university deans live. On the one hand, you are likely to
have fewer staff to help you accomplish your responsibilities. You know more of
the players on your campus; there are fewer of them, and campus political affairs
may be less complicated. Your constituents comprise a less specialized cadre of
academic folk than if you were, say, dean of the school of engineering at a large
university.

On the other hand, your responsibilities may be more varied—all academic spe-
cies report to you—and you may be required to be part of the governing team,
part of the CEO's office rather than a branch manager concerned to protect turf
and secure assets for your troupe regardless of the cost to other divisions. While
you may have charge of a wider scope of activity than a university dean, you are
also likely to have less autonomy, especially in fund raising, than deans have at many
large mega-universities. If the chief executive officer is arguably the real chief advancement (or development) officer at any college or university, you are less likely
at a small institution to see yourself as a quasi-autonomous advancement officer
for your school, division, or area, bearing some of the responsibility and glory of
the president.

Because of your special role in the institution, your function in raising funds may
be different from that of your colleagues in bigger places. It may be useful to in-
spect five areas:

- creating a relationship with the development office;
- devising ideas for projects to be funded;

- establishing a system to make use of available staff;
- working with donors; and
- working with faculty on fund-raising projects.

Dividing responsibilities: Your relationship with the development office

Because of the heavy demands from many quarters made on your time, you may find your contact with your fund-raising counterpart, the chief advancement officer (CAO), limited to scheduled meetings of the president's cabinet. Both you and the CAO must prevent this: You will both benefit enormously if you can schedule periodic meetings.

By meeting every two weeks or even once a month, you can reaffirm ground rules you've established. More important, you can teach each other about your cultures, so often intersecting, so often clashing. (The fact that your CAO colleague went to an institution like yours doesn't mean he or she knows how academics think. You and the CAO may describe academia in the same terms and mean opposite things. You may think of asking for a gift as a half-hour process while the CAO sees it as a continuum stretching over months or years, with dozens of steps.) Each of you will increase your respect for the other's hegemony and will begin to understand how differently institutional politics shapes your actions and limits your possibilities.

As you work and talk together, you and the CAO will learn that each of you can produce suggestions, with sources in your own experience, that will affect the academic life of the institution. Each suggestion may make sense; each may have the capacity to improve the school's impact on students. Yet those suggestions are not subject to consensus or to evaluation by voting democratically, for you as academic officer have policy-making rights not shared by the CAO. (You're likely to find that the CAO understands this well; he or she may already tell development staffers that they cannot accept gifts that affect academic or curricular policy without decanal approval. But if not, this is a lesson you'll have to teach.) While each of you may come up with ideas, you are the one who decides whether a particular idea makes sense at your institution.

You carry more weight in making another kind of decision too. Let's say you and the CAO have agreed that seven projects merit support. Each deserves attention. Which comes first? The CAO may argue compellingly that Project A should come first because a donor is ready to fund it, while Project G has to come last because it will take much work to find and cultivate prospects. But you may see that Project D has the greatest urgency, Project G must precede B, F, C, and E in that order, and Project A could easily wait. Both of you have to understand what impact your decisions will have, you have to weigh competing priorities—and you will almost certainly have to involve the president in any difficult decisions.

As you teach each other, discuss complementary and competing suggestions, and cooperate in establishing priorities, you will find that your professional relationship has a natural rhythm; you will find yourselves both giving and taking orders, taking command or yielding it to the other as the situation demands.

Coming up with ideas and testing them

You and others may generate ideas that will foster your institution's growth and development. You, your faculty colleagues, the CAO, and the development staff—all would be well advised to pretend that anything is possible and, at the same time, to assume that nothing is possible.

First you must pretend that any new idea can work, that it can produce wonderful results with no negative impact. Why? Because each of us, as an administrative officer, has turf to protect; every change is a threat, and if we stop at the moment an idea is born to assess its prospects, we are likely to kill it with concern. You may despair of its surviving ferocious political battles in faculty committees; the CAO may think no donor is likely to find it appealing; for the moment, you must both ignore such worries. Right now you are both caught up in the wonder of the new idea, and you must strive to understand its implications.

Thoroughly intoxicated by the splendor of the idea (whatever its original source), you must now assume nothing is possible, or practically nothing. You must imagine your institution without the benefit of what you have contrived—without the enticing scholarship program, the professorship that will let you break new ground with a new audience, the laboratory that will challenge your students to new heights of scientific understanding. By plumbing these depths, you understand the real cost of ignoring this dream; its absence—not the difficulty of campus politics or the hardship of appealing to the proper donor—will be the real cost your institution will pay by not going forward.

Now that you, the CAO, and other members of the senior administrative team comprehend the costs of acting and of failing to act, you can weigh your ideas and put them in priority order.

Creating a regular program for support

You and your colleagues in academic administration will have inherited, or quickly established, routine connections with the registrar, the financial office, the dean of students, the president, and the chair of the academic affairs committee of the board of trustees. These offices extend your world; they enable you to accomplish your goals and let you do more than you could by yourself. Yet you are likely to assume that you have no routine connection with your colleague in charge of institutional advancement.

Don't.

While coexisting in adversarial roles can comfort in hard times ("Of course we can't do what we really need to do here; the cretins in development don't raise enough money"), an inimical relationship prevents progress and limits your power.

You will accomplish more as dean if the CAO is on your team because the CAO will extend fund-raising potential by using your strengths.

Let me repeat what I suggested earlier: See each other regularly, as often as possible.

The reason? You will come to respect each other's ideas if you sample them often. Gradually, even the oddest views of the world can become comprehensible, if not natural; even the dean and the development chief can become less of polar opposites if they talk often. (Of course, not all deans and CAOs are diametrically opposed in their view of the institution; but their cultures are not naturally familiar. The dean may think that all development officers play golf twice weekly on workday afternoons, and the fund raiser may believe the dean can think only obscure thoughts expressed in polysyllabic density. Both can be wrong.)

Perhaps equally important, although more mundane: If you talk often, you will come to exchange information. You will both know whether you're on schedule in getting a proposal finished; you will have to reveal whether you made the cultivation phone call you promised to make; you will share information on changes in schedule. You will, in short, make more progress working together than you do working separately.

You will make progress in other ways too. You will suggest to each other possibilities for support to be researched. You will sharpen each other's vision of the proposal you're working on, making the text more persuasive. (You will find that colloquy produces new ideas too, ideas that can't really be credited to either of you; they leap forth unbidden when you talk.) You'll remind each other of reports that need to go to donors, and the CAO will help you to understand that no facet of fund raising is more important than stewardship.

Finally, you will deepen your appreciation of your political surroundings. It's said that campus politics are so ferocious because the spoils are so small; you and your CAO colleague may find yourselves immobilized by ferocious political turmoil. You can minimize that possibility by teaching each other, by pointing to foes lurking behind the shrubbery. It may not be the announcement of failure that brings you to your knees, but rather its timing or the person to whom you first mention it; and great success in grantsmanship may cause not appreciation but newly unsatisfied expectation if not displayed wisely. You can help each other toward that wisdom.

Working with donors

Faculty members, I find, often think of development as a process of taking orders, rather like a Dairy Queen clerk at a higher level. You, as an academic officer of uncommon sophistication, have grown beyond that callow view; but even you may not recognize how much effort over how long a time may be required to produce gifts of magnitude.

The difficulty for all of us in colleges is that our best ideas proclaim their value and their immediacy at the same moment; we want them now so they may do the greatest good. There are two impediments to their becoming real, and one—the collegiate political process—is more obvious to academic thinkers than the other—

the difficulty of paying for yet another valuable project.

Even as you contemplate a valuable change in curriculum, in staffing, or in facilities, you think at the same time of how to make it happen: you know what committees you must cajole, what chairs to shift, what sops to toss.

You may not realize, however, that funding sources do not often lend themselves to the same kind of political manipulation. They can depart quickly if they think themselves used, and therefore they must come to feel themselves part of the operation of the academic institution. This doesn't happen quickly; there is a direct correlation, usually, between the importance of a gift and the length of its gestation.

Perhaps we all recognize instinctively that agricultural metaphors govern much of our thinking in fund raising. Fishing for dollars produces little for the effort expended; simply dropping a line usually produces little, and the big fish caught so simply is as rare as a big lottery win. Plucking at least aims at the visible; if we look carefully, we can see the largest ears and pick them first. (This metaphor applies most obviously to annual giving, but it's useful in some capital gift operations too.) The most important philanthropy, however, results from sowing, cultivating, and harvesting the well-planted crop.

As we seek the harvest, the most important point to remember is that it's their money. Potential donors own the money, and they have the right to determine how it's to be used. The greater the person, the grander the vision of which he or she is capable; the grander the vision, the greater the gift. But that grand vision must belong to the donor, not the solicitor; and while the solicitor may have suggested the substance of that vision, ultimately the donor must make it his or her own.

You and the CAO may—*must*—work together to foster this breadth of vision. While the donor may have a nascent idea of what life can accomplish, you as the academic chief can help put flesh on a skeleton; you can provide words of complexity, sophistication, and compelling persuasion that make the vision real.

Just as it's not easy to take the germ of an idea and turn it into a grand vision, it's also not easy to become the familiar confidant whose wisdom and insight are so captivating that they can be trusted. To create the kind of relationship that leads to great gifts for great purposes demands work and devotion on your part, work and devotion with uncertain rewards.

In other words, you must yourself be a big person if you wish to foster big things in others. Your satisfaction must come from the value of the task, not from the value of the reward.

If that sounds like pious catechism, rest easy that even at levels that produce only significant (if not grand) gifts, you can help cultivate the harvest. No donor gives who feels an unsatisfactory relationship with his or her college, and you—second only to the president—have the potential to create an abiding and productive relationship.

When it's time for solicitation, you may once again claim primacy. The person who asks for the gift should be the one who stands highest in the eyes of the donor. For the prospect capable of a very large gift, that's most often the president, the chair of the board, or the campaign chair. But relationship is all, and sometimes it will be you who are closest to the donor. In that case *you* must ask.

The important word here is "ask"—not suggest, imply, or hint, but "ask." Remember that donors rarely give more than they're asked for, and if they remember no specific amount, they haven't been asked at all. You must ask for a specific gift.

You should, however, couch your request more in the language of benefit and accomplishment than in the language of funds. What you ask for is the power to help young people, to provide the laboratory in which they will work or the books they need to find in the library. When prospects see—and smell—the benefit, the money will seem incidental. But they must know what money you need.

I have hinted earlier that stewardship claims title to the most important development process. So it does. In development parlance, stewardship is the process of thanking and rethanking the donor. Some one has said that an important gift deserves seven sets of thanks; perhaps so. Certainly it deserves more than one. You should add your voice to the throng thanking the donor for a significant gift.

More important to the donor and to the stewardship process, you should make sure the donor always remembers that you always think of the benefit the gift has wrought. The donor must know each year that his gift reaches students in need, that her endowed professorship enables a valued teacher to perform important scholarship. If the gift was for a specific academic function—the library, a fund for faculty development, a professorship—it's likely that you or your decanal colleagues will be responsible for principal acts of stewardship.

Don't ignore that responsibility. The most likely donor is the one who has given before, and the one who has given before is most likely to give again when he or she understands viscerally that what has been done in the past lives still in the life of the institution. You have the power to create that recognition and to create the possibility of subsequent gifts; you have the power by inaction to render successive benefaction unlikely.

Working with faculty

We have spoken above of the dangers inherent in adversarial relationships between you and your advancement colleagues. Here let's think more about what might be referred to as the diplomacy of expectation.

As chief academic officer you seek to foster brilliance and inspiration among your faculty. Their brilliance and their inspired performance can lead to tenure, even to fame. What fans their brilliance? Often, the promise of support for their ideas.

Here's where danger lies, for you by yourself cannot often promise that support. In the pages above, we've contemplated the advantages of making the CAO your teammate. While you and the CAO should always see each other as comrades, from time to time you may find it useful to employ a "good cop, bad cop" scenario. Just as the CAO may have to corral the grandiose ideas of an untutored donor by reminding him or her that the dean must approve all ideas that have academic impact, so you may find it useful to use the specter of the advancement operation, with all its arcana, to quell the ardor of a faculty member whose idea carried to fruition might damage the reputation of the institution.

116

At the same time, you must engage the faculty as a source of ideas. Virtually all ideas that will enable your college to face its uncertain future will come from your faculty colleagues, if not from you as chief among them. They must recognize, as you have by now, that value comes from pretending that any idea is possible. You must suffer many foolish ideas gladly in order to find the few that will let your college excel.

Subsequently, you must engage some of your faculty colleagues in sowing, cultivating, and harvesting—although, as you might expect, their greatest assistance will come in cultivation. Not all faculty members will be able to see beyond their needs to the needs of donors, but you will learn to identify these gems and treasure them. (They will probably also be your best committee members and valued leaders within the faculty.) They may be the faculty members most valued as stewards, too, for they may ascend to the prized named professorships.

You will make certain that all faculty members who benefit from the munificence of donors remind those donors regularly of the value of their gifts. This may consist of annual reports from named professors, periodic news from a dean about the value of an endowed program for faculty development, or the librarian's lists of books purchased through an endowed library fund. While your CAO colleague may remind you to do these stewardship tasks, he or she cannot perform them as well as you can.

Finally, you will have the unenviable job of reminding your faculty colleagues to be grateful, to remember that they have no claim on the wealth of others, that each of us needs succor from someone else. I hope it will not seem crass to remind you that such humility can breed gifts.

The dean as advancement officer

You will have discovered, as you read through these pages, that you have been asked to do much of what the CAO does. To be sure, you do not have responsibility for creating and managing a development program, supervising donor research, creating or maintaining a donor tracking system, or building liaison with outside constituencies through public relations or publications. But you have been asked to think about how gifts come about and why people make those gifts, and you have been urged to become part of the advancement team.

In a small academic institution, where everyone is pressed to go beyond his or her special field of expertise, to adopt yet another set of responsibilities may seem impossible, the request to do so cavalier. Yet in a large sense, at a small college you have a great power to influence all the life of your institution through your willingness to persuade others of the value of your case. And who can do it better than you?

I wish to express my gratitude for invaluable advice in preparing this chapter to John Orr Dwyer, vice president for academic services, Thiel College; R. Stanton Hales, vice president for academic affairs, The College of Wooster; Elizabeth McKinsey, dean of the college, Carleton College; and David Spadafora, dean of the faculty, Lake Forest College.

Chapter 16

Health Sciences Fund Raising

Linda G. Steckley
Assistant Dean for Development and Alumni Relations
School of Law
New York University
(Formerly Assistant Vice President
Development for Medical Affairs
University of Miami School of Medicine)

A t the ground-breaking ceremony for a magnificent, university-affiliated comprehensive cancer center, the principal donor was being thanked for his generosity when he unexpectedly took exception: "On the contrary," he replied, "*I* thank *you*. My money could not have the same impact if it were not for this university and this outstanding medical center. We have the opportunity with this cancer center to save or to improve the lives of thousands of people. There is no way that I could possibly accomplish that on my own."

The donor had lost one parent to cancer, the other to heart disease. He had recently moved to the area from another part of the country. Because of his new proximity to the university and its medical center, the donor knew he could maintain a high level of involvement with the project that he had made possible. He was enthusiastic about the thought of following the construction of the facility, getting to know the staff physicians, and learning more about their research.

This incident highlights key differences between fund raising for the health sciences and fund raising for other academic areas. What is significant here is that prior to the time he made the gift, neither the donor nor any member of his family had any allegiance to the university or its medical center. They didn't even have any ties to the community.

His decision was a purely emotional one. "My parents are standing here beside me," he said at the ground-breaking. "This is for them."

This kind of special constituency is one of the elements that distinguishes health sciences fund raising from other academic development. Health sciences fund raising doesn't depend on alumni, parents, or sports boosters, but on committed individuals with a vision that includes your institution.

Of critical importance is the ability of the dean and development officer to identify the special constituencies and to be sensitive to their individual needs and to their differences.

Special constituency fund raising

The potential sources for fund raising in the health sciences are almost unlimited. They range from volunteer groups at the medical center to committed citizens with no previous ties to the institution, from former patients of the hospital to faculty doctors who are intimately involved with life-and-death dramas on a daily basis, from health industry corporations to the school's alumni.

Whoever the constituent is, the dean's task and that of the faculty physicians is to build a relationship, not solely to seek money. When there is a compelling case for giving, you won't find it difficult to develop donor relationships. Problems often arise, however, because of the variety of interests and priorities of the donors. Each has his or her own opinions and attitudes regarding the appropriate direction for the institution. This puts enormous pressure on the dean and the chief development officer in a medical center to encourage involvement while at the same time resisting the donor's desire to determine policy and direction.

The best way to discourage donor involvement in decision making is to have a clear and well-communicated planning process for medical programs. This is not to say that you can't be receptive to opportunities presented through the offer of a leadership gift, but in most cases a gift of that magnitude comes only after a period of involvement during which the dean has made sure that the prospective donor is fully informed about the mission and the dreams of the medical center.

Identifying potential donors

Every American medical school has a relationship with one or more hospitals. Some are public facilities; some are private. There is bound to be competition between the hospital and the medical center to attract grateful patients' philanthropic dollars. In reality these entities are interdependent, and the success or failure of one has a direct bearing on the other.

The advantage held by the university medical center is that the hospital doctors are members of the university faculty. People often give to medical schools so that when they are faced with a medical need, they will have access to the best doctors and the most current research. In this context, their charitable contributions might be seen as a form of insurance.

Some medical schools have a development staff person who serves as the patient representative or liaison. This person facilitates the appointment process and checks on patients' needs. When a donor, or known potential donor, to the medical school needs medical services, the patient representative facilitates the appointment process and checks on patients' needs. When a donor, or known potential donor, to the medical school needs medical services, the patient representative facilitates the appointment process and checks on the patient's needs. It's important to maintain a balance here. While the development staff should show concern for a patient and his or her family, they don't want to appear to be "vultures," interested only in the family wealth. The key is the relationship that develops between the physician, the donor, and the donor's family.

In many communities the dean of the medical school is a much-revered individual whose concern is deeply appreciated by the patient and his or her family. The development officer serves as the dean's partner, the primary communicator, keeping the dean informed about who is being treated and seeking feedback from patients about the quality of hospital care. Whether a patient becomes a donor often depends on how he or she is treated: Do doctors and nurses respect the patient's dignity? Are the institution's systems user-friendly? Do doctors share all pertinent information about the patient's condition with appropriate family members?

The ability to control the level of customer service differs from one medical center to another. Some hospitals do a much better job than others in promoting sensitivity to customer needs. The number of university hospital affiliations and the culture of the hospital also affect whether you will find it easy or very hard indeed to raise gifts from former patients.

When the university owns the hospital, the dean and department chairs can have a considerable impact on the culture of the hospital. It is the people at the top of the organization who are able to establish the kind of environment that is obsessive about its attention to the needs of customers. Current efforts to develop quality management programs in medical centers may do more to augment development efforts than anything else, except for the basic requirement of assuring quality medical care.

Relationship with central development

Other units of the university are likely to be the medical center's chief competitors for donor dollars. Traditionally, communication between the central development offices of the university and offices of medical development has been grudging. Deans of other academic areas envy the apparent ease of raising major gifts for the health sciences. No other unit of the institution—except athletics—can cross into the larger community for support with the facility of the medical center. No matter what school a donor attended at the institution, in times of illness—times of greatest need and vulnerability—he or she turns to the medical center. Thus, it is important that everyone on the "team" (medical school dean, faculty, and development staff) makes a genuine effort to cooperate with the rest of the institution, while still working to protect and promote the interests of the health sciences.

In many cases the medical side of the institution produces the majority of the university's annual gift dollars as well as the bulk of major gifts and estate gifts.

While the dean and doctors may sometimes feel that increased autonomy would serve the long-term interests of the medical school, it's important to remember that donors depend on the credibility and stability of the university to ensure the value of their investment in the medical center.

Openness and negotiation between the central university development office and medical center development work better than secretiveness and distrust. Whether via a computer system or through periodic prospect discussions, it is important to share information about current prospects, solicitation strategies, and projected timeframes. Prospects are people too, and they have a variety of interests. Many donors value highly the opportunity their gift brings them to become involved with the university and enjoy its many exciting programs and benefits.

Theoretically any unit of the institution has the right to cultivate any prospect, but the medical development office should always clear any major gift solicitation through a central process. When the institution is preparing a proposal, be sure to include options in a number of areas of interest to the potential donor.

When the development staff brief the president, dean, or key volunteer for a solicitation, they should discuss all areas of possible commitment. The last thing anyone needs is to be less than fully informed during a solicitation, and this is particularly important in the case of the president, dean, or member of the board of trustees—the people most likely to be involved in a major gift effort. Everything possible should be done to ensure the success of the request.

Doctors

The constituent group closest to the institution and most knowledgeable about its critical needs is the physician faculty. A number of the country's most prominent medical centers view their physicians as the primary source of gift revenue. Many faculty members, however, believe they are already making a substantial contribution to the institution by working as academic/research physicians rather than going into a much more lucrative private practice.

Faculty physicians need and desire the same care and nurturing as the school's most important external donors. The best way to help a doctor become a donor is to involve him or her in the process of raising money for the medical center. For example, when a new chair was appointed to a major department at a large university medical school, the young doctor had a dream of creating a world-renown institute in his discipline. The dean and the university Board of Trustees fully supported the project, and the initial cost was set at approximately $15 million. The chair and his development officer identified a few leadership prospects, but, as yet, no gifts were actually committed.

The first lesson for the new chair was to experience the cultivation process first-hand and learn how it leads to a solicitation. The young doctor and his wife took to the social aspects of cultivation like naturals. His charm and genuine commitment to the project were contagious. The lead prospect was a foundation established by the family of a woman who suffred the debilitating condition that the doctor was working to cure. Her son was a graduate of the university, although the family had moved to another state many years earlier. The doctor was able to establish a warm friendship with the son and his wife; the concept of the institute was of interest to the family; everything seemed to be in place for a successful ask. The proposal was submitted, but it was turned down. The doctor was incredulous. What had gone wrong?

Often a philanthropic decision is difficult to understand. In this case, the foundation was committed to supporting medical efforts in another part of the country. The woman's son could not persuade the other members of the foundation board to alter this policy. As disappointing as the outcome was, it taught the physician a valuable lesson in the vagaries of fund raising: Unlike laboratory experiments, A plus B does not always equal C.

The doctor also realized that his own commitment had to go beyond words and the fancy drawings of a proposed building. He coud not ask others to do something that he was not willing to do himself. He became a donor, not only to his own area, but also to other areas of the medical center that had a direct impact on his interests. His firsthand experience as a fund raiser resulted in his own financial commitment.

There is no quick way to speed the learning curve of physicians trying to comprehend development. The key to success is to enable them to have the kind of fund-raising involvement that will develop these faculty members into a donor base.

Medical alumni and the annual fund

In long-established medical schools, the alumni form the base of annual support, just as the alumni provide the foundation of giving in the college of arts and sciences, the business school, and the law school. If the institution is a young, private medical school or a public university medical center that does not have a long tradition of organized fund raising, the annual fund may not have developed to its full potential. This is a critically important aspect of the health sciences development program as well as the primary avenue of support for medical alumni.

It is not, however, necessary to reinvent the wheel. The medical center can piggyback onto the university's annual fund. This usually makes sense, even if the timing is not exactly right. Medical development can use university annual fund publications and promotional material whenever possible. The medical development staff should be involved in the planning of the university's annual fund program, making sure to include medical news as part of the case for support. Recognize that the medical center is frequently the jewel in the university's crown and can be used to enhance the image of other areas.

Most health science centers, including schools of nursing and dentistry as well as medicine, use a combination of direct mail and telephone contact to develop annual gifts at levels of less than $1,000. The sequence of the approach doesn't seem to matter as much as establishing some sort of tradition. If the school uses a phone campaign, schedule it for the same time each year. Prerequisites to success are accurate records and prompt follow-up. Callers can't make contact unless they have phone numbers and the numbers are correct. Mail that isn't delivered to the right address won't be read. People who make pledges will not fulfill them if they don't receive pledge cards. The successful sequence of the steps in an annual fund is dependent upon accurate and timely data.

The role of the dean and faculty is to be visibly supportive of the annual fund, often the primary source of the unrestricted funds that enable the development office to function. In many cases the annual fund also provides the funding for student loans and financial aid. If a letter of solicitation is the first step in the annual fund process, it can go out over the dean's signature. This letter might be in the form of an update about the school, mentioning highlights of accomplishments during the past year and specific goals for the current year. It should be warm and personal in tone and make the alumnus want to invest in the mission of the medical school.

Another successful approach is to invite a much-loved professor or associate dean to serve as honorary chair of the annual fund—the dean for student affairs, for example, or a professor of one of the core courses that everyone takes. If this person has been with the school for many years, he or she will have touched the lives of many students.

One institution sent out postcards with a photograph of a beloved associate dean talking on the telephone and the message: "I'll be calling YOU!" The card announced the dates of the phone campaign and the importance of raising dollars to support student financial aid. Although the dean could not make all the calls himself, the photo stirred memories that gave the volunteer alumni callers a starting point for conversation about the needs of the school. The campaign was the most successful ever.

If faculty members who are also alumni are willing to spend an evening participating in making calls, they can help generate enthusiasm on the part of other volunteers. Some schools use alumni volunteers to make calls; others pay medical students in cash or credit vouchers; still others use paid, trained telemarketing specialists. Each approach has advantages, but using professionals puts the activity outside of dean or faculty involvement and could possibly raise the cost as well.

Planning and implementation of the annual fund should be staff-driven. The dean can participate by visiting the phone campaign site to thank the volunteer callers and by making sure letters of solicitation and acknowledgment go out over his or her signature. But the dean's time and efforts should focus on larger leadership-level gifts.

The long-term value of the annual fund is that it establishes communication with alumni over the years. And it is from these regular contributors that major gifts and estate gifts will eventually come. If you don't establish and nurture a relationship with these faithful givers, you are unlikely to receive any major gifts from them in the future.

One of the greatest challenges facing medical schools is to bring alumni back to campus. Because of the highly specialized nature of the profession, doctors want to meet and talk with other doctors in their field or specialty. Medical school alumni usually don't have a strong sense of loyalty to the larger university and are not likely to return for a major athletic event or homecoming. Reunions for a medical school class often take place at a ski resort or on a cruise ship where social interaction prevails, rather than back on campus. Nevertheless, reunions, wherever they take place, can be an effective way to ensure the continuation of alumni relationships. For example, you could combine the reunion with a continuing education program. The development staff can provide support for the class reunion committee, with the dean and invited members of the faculty attending. Alumni who participate in these events can become key contacts in the ongoing effort to identify class members with giving potential. A system of class representatives comprising an alumni board of directors often facilitates this kind of involvement.

The dean and chief development officer can decide to expand the medical center's annual fund to include friends and grateful patients who have made gifts in the past. If someone has cared enough to make a gift once, chances are that he or she still feels a sense of commitment. Remember that people rarely give unless they are asked, and the objective is to encourage one-time contributors to include the medical center in their yearly charitable giving. Although these gifts may be relatively small, when you have hundreds of them, they begin to add up.

The most frequent initial approach to nonalumni is through the mail. You can combine a written appeal to friends of the medical center with distribution of the annual report or the brochure describing the latest medical developments at the center. It can be as simple as a straightforward request from the dean or a well-known physician. The key is to give the prospect a sense of the importance of the work of the medical center, the impact of its presence on the community, and the ever-present need for contributed dollars.

Trustees and advisory committees

The dean and the chief development officer of a large university medical center were reviewing names of members of the university board of trustees to identify potential donors to the medical school when they realized that nearly every trustee had needed the services of a faculty physician during the past few years—either for himself or herself or for a family member. There is no better precedent for giving, particularly for people like board members who are already involved with the institution. But even board members need to be asked.

Start with board members who have received medical care themselves, and make sure they understand the mission of the medical center; discuss with them the quality of care they received and the concerns of the physicians and hospital staff. Be sure they understand the important research in progress and possible breakthroughs in treatment. It is then the job of the dean or the faculty physician who attended the board member during the illness to ask him or her to help in raising funds for the medical center.

Trustees are on the board in the first place because of their broad spheres of influence and the credentials they bring to the governance and policy-setting of the university. These same qualities mark them for potential leadership in fund-raising efforts for the institution.

Don't, however, make trustees feel that their financial commitment is an obligation attendant to appointment to the board. Rather, the appointment should give them the opportunity to understand the work of the university and the medical center and should form the foundation for a dynamic relationship. Again, it is the dean who is the chief spokesperson in describing to the trustee this unique opportunity for leadership. With background information from the development office on previous involvement and level of giving, you can work with the development office to design a strategy for approaching and involving each trustee.

Involvement of a university trustee must be meaningful, such as interaction with medical students who have taken on a community health project for the homeless or for migrant workers. Work by faculty physicians in the fields of drug abuse, AIDS, teenage motherhood, or other areas of public concern affords opportunities for a legitimate role to be played by a community leader who is also a trustee.

Just as in the case of the department chair, the trustee should be a donor before becoming a solicitor of gifts. When he or she reaches a sufficient level of involvement, the dean or a physician who has become close to the family can make the request for financial commitment.

If the medical center is in a major campaign, the campaign organization should include a number of trustees. Perhaps a key member of the board serves as chair, with four to six other trustees as vice chairs. Trustees can recruit additional influential community members to serve on the campaign committee. If the project is a relatively small, area-specific campaign, you may need only one or two trustee leaders. All, however, should have had some involvement with the medical center before they assume a direct leadership position.

For individuals with leadership skills who may not yet be on the university board, the advisory board can also serve to provide involvement. Usually comprised of individuals who have been personally touched by the medical program in some way, this board does not have responsibility for governance of the unit. An effective advisory board, in addition to providing valuable counsel and planning direction, can also lead implementation of special projects. Leadership on an advisory board can serve as an excellent training for future membership on the board of trustees.

An advisory board is usually established for a particular unit or center within the medical center. The dean and development officer should try to manage the membership so that key corporations and sectors of the community are represented. For example, a medical center burn unit wanted to form an advisory board that would generate fund-raising efforts far beyond what the doctor and the small development staff could undertake. The new board included not only influential people who had some personal experience with the treatment of burn victims, but also a member of the local fire department and an executive from the electrical company. These people had an obvious professional interest in the prevention of burns and the care of burn victims.

The fund-raising strategy incorporated substantive input from the dean, burn center director, key members of the advisory board, the chief development officer for the medical center, and the development officer assigned to work with the burn center. The plan, which was to be implemented over several years, included both event-oriented activities and major gift cultivation and solicitation. Although deans and faculty members quickly learn that a higher level of funding can be obtained through major gift solicitation than through labor-intensive events, fund-raising events are important in heightening community awareness of the project and in identifying people with an interest in the area.

Working with volunteer groups

The board of directors or advisory board is just one form of volunteer group that can support a medical center. Probably the most important difference between standard academic fund raising and health sciences fund raising is that there are many more volunteer organizations that support a medical center. So much can be done by volunteers at a medical center that most hospitals today have a coordinator of volunteer services.

The development office has to be be very careful in screening the objectives of volunteer groups and providing advice, counsel, and support to those with a clear fund-raising purpose. There is, however, always the danger that if you give too much support to a few demanding individuals, they may begin to view the development office as their own personal support staff. The chief development officer must maintain constant communication with staff about the expectations of volunteers and establish clear guidelines as to what the office can provide and what the group must do for itself.

Occasionally the dean will need to intervene in a difficult situation. For example, an active volunteer fund-raising organization was nearing completion of a commitment to one department of an urban medical school. The group had been so successful that a number of doctors were hoping that their area would be the object of the group's next effort. As a major lobbying movement got under way, the medical development staff found itself caught in the middle. Staff cannot take sides in advocating one area over another. The dean stepped in, mediated among the doctors, and went back to the volunteers with an explanation of why one of the departments was most appropriate for their members' attention.

It is vitally important that the dean and faculty members who benefit from the fund-raising efforts of volunteer organizations publicly recognize and thank the individuals and groups. Each major gift should be recognized in an appropriate fashion, while the combined efforts of all the groups can be formally acknowledged once a year through a luncheon, a dinner, a gala, or other event, depending on the custom of the community.

Be sure the university president is aware of the contributions of the volunteer groups and has ample opportunity to say his or her own "thank you." University publications, as well as those of the medical school, should prominently feature the contributions of individuals and groups to medical programs. Appreciation from the larger university community can be strong reinforcement for continued work. Again, the message is that the medical school does not stand alone, but is a dominant component of the total institution.

The development partnership

The dean almost always has the ability to select the chief development officer for the medical center. Unfortunately, while the dean may be accustomed to weighing the qualifications of physicians, educators, and scholars, he or she is not usually as experienced at evaluating the credentials of fund raisers. After thoroughly reviewing the professional qualifications of the candidates, the dean may well consider the "chemistry" he or she feels with the various applicants. This is a key factor in a successful working relationship. The best dean/development officer partnerships always have a sense of shared purpose, an understanding that can be communicated with a minimum of conversation. The development officer must understand the dean's mission for the institution and concur with these objectives to the point that they become his or her own.

The dean must feel that the development officer is a key member of his or her staff, privy to confidential information about pending problems and organizational accomplishments. The development officer must be a person of sensitivity and discretion, knowing when to speak on behalf of the dean and when to remain silent. The development officer serves as primary liaison to the rest of the university administration as well as the larger external community. He or she must be knowledgeable about the work of the faculty and able to translate it into language comprehensible to the layperson. The chief development officer needs to share a contagious enthusiasm and commitment with the staff and prospective donors.

Together, the dean and chief development officer have the ability to determine the legacy of a particular period of time in the history of the institution. They can develop relationships that will produce funding for the future greatness of the medical center. All of the dreams of a dean will come to nothing without adequate financial resources.

We sometimes forget that raising support for compelling medical programs is a privilege afforded to few. What more meaningful opportunities exist than to ensure the quality education of future physicians or to support the research leading to cures for dreaded diseases?

The men and women who are leading America's medical schools in a time of tremendous pressure on health care systems are courageous individuals. They are also people of vision with a sense of the great opportunity they have to make the world a better place. The men and women who support them as fund raisers have a vital role to play. They can help to make the dreams a reality.

We sometimes scoff at the euphemism "development," but it implies a broad understanding of a society that requires the building of relationships and the acquiring of financial investment to accomplish major goals. Deans and their partners, the faculty and development officers, can guide people with wealth to see the potential for good that can be achieved through their joint efforts. Together they can build a program of lasting value that neither could build alone.

About the Editor

Mary Kay Murphy

Mary Kay Murphy, editor of *Building Bridges: Fund Raising for Deans, Faculty, and Development Officers,* is a long-time CASE volunteer and currently serves as associate vice president for development at Oglethorpe University in Atlanta.

She served as chair of CASE District III during the preparation and publication of this book, from 1991-93. In July 1992 she became a member of the CASE Board of Trustees. She serves through 1995 on the Trusteeship, the Membership and Marketing, and the District Service Committees of the Board.

During her development career, she has worked closely with 18 deans in the three predominant higher education models: the German scientific model at the Georgia Institute of Technology; the British undergraduate model at Oglethorpe University; and the American land-grant model at The University of Georgia.

She holds a Ph.D. in Higher Education Administration from Georgia State University and an M.Ed. in English and Education Research from Emory University. In 1989 she edited the CASE publication, *Cultivating Foundation Support for Education.* She has written over 150 articles on education and fund raising, has chaired five regional and national CASE conferences, given over 100 presentations on fund raising and development, and has been an active Board member of the National Society of Fund Raising Executives as well as Georgia Coordinator of the American Council on Education's National Identification Program for Women in Higher Education Administration

She is listed in *Who's Who of American Women* and *Who's Who in the South and Southwest.*

NOTES

NOTES

NOTES

NOTES